PUB STROLLS IN

NORFOLK

Will Martin

COUNTRYSIDE BOOKS
NEWBURY BERKSHIRE

First published 2001
© Will Martin 2001

COUNTRYSIDE BOOKS
3 Catherine Road
Newbury, Berkshire

To view our complete range of books,
please visit us at
www.countrysidebooks.co.uk

ISBN 1 85306 672 9

*For my parents, Reg and Win, with whom
I enjoyed many happy hours walking.
And for my wife, Lynne, who was a good
companion on these strolls.*

Photographs by the author
Maps by the author and redrawn by
Gelder design and mapping

Designed by Graham Whiteman

Produced through MRM Associates Ltd., Reading
Printed by Woolnough Bookbinding Ltd., Irthlingborough

Contents

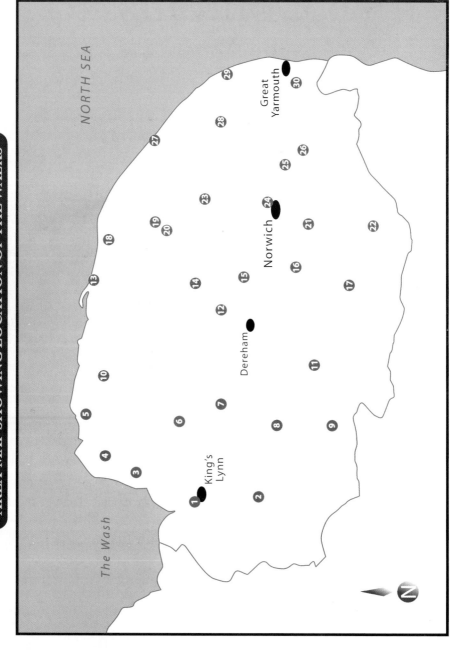

AREA MAP SHOWING LOCATION OF THE WALKS

The Wash

NORTH SEA

King's
Lynn

Dereham

Norwich

Great
Yarmouth

N

WALK

PUBLISHER'S NOTE

We hope that you obtain considerable enjoyment from this book; great care has been taken in its preparation. However, changes of landlord and actual closures are sadly not uncommon. Likewise, although at the time of publication all routes followed public rights of way or permitted paths, diversion orders can be made and permissions withdrawn.

We cannot, of course, be held responsible for such diversion orders and any inaccuracies in the text which result from these or any other changes to the routes nor any damage which might result from walkers trespassing on private property. We are anxious though that all details covering the walks and the pubs are kept up to date and would therefore welcome information from readers which would be relevant to future editions.

The sketch maps accompanying each walk are not always to scale and are intended to guide you to the starting point and give a simple but accurate idea of the route to be taken. For those who like the benefit of detailed maps, we recommend that you arm yourself with the relevant Ordnance Survey map in the Landranger series.

This book of short circular walks based on good pubs, serving good food, is designed to give a flavour of the sometimes under-estimated pleasures of the Norfolk country-side and its long, eventful history.

For a start, there is a much greater variety of landscape than the newcomer might imagine. From the wave-scoured shingle beaches and bird-rich saltmarshes of the coast, via reed-fringed broads and lush farmland to the conifer forests and heaths of Breckland, there is a world of change. But just as important as the features of the physical landscape are the more subtle and maybe sometimes taken-for-granted joys that Norfolk has to offer – chief among which is the sky. The vast, ever-changing skyscape dominates Norfolk walking to provide a wealth of interest in its shifting cloud patterns, stunning sunsets and distant storms, but above all else to give a sense of openness and freedom that truly lifts the spirits.

Norfolk wildlife, too, is a major factor in the enjoyment of walking here. It will be obvious that one of my main loves is birdwatching, and for the variety, as well as the sheer numbers of birds, this is one of the best places in Britain. Deer can often be seen too, especially the tiny muntjac.

What else? Churches – I have men-tioned a lot of them, not only because Norfolk has so many magnificent examples but because, in a flat landscape, they are more prominent than elsewhere, always on view as you walk and welcoming you back to the beginning.

In such a heavily cultivated county, crops play a major part in the scene and here again there are perhaps under-estimated pleasures. An acre of sugar beet is a pretty boring thing, I grant you, but how about a field of barley near harvest-time, rippling in the wind with that lovely reddish tinge? Or a field of linseed with its drifts of delicate blue?

And finally, since this is a book of pub strolls, there are the splendid, historic pubs of Norfolk with their excellent local beers and wide choice of food using fresh local ingredients. I am sure you will find a welcome here. With regard to car parking, on some walks I have noted that parking is only 'with permission' of the landlord. On others, where I have not said this, landlords are happy for patrons to park without asking although, in the interests of common courtesy, it might be prudent to let the landlord know your intentions before setting out on the walk.

Most of the walks cross farmland at some point and so the obvious countryside courtesies are important, such as closing gates behind you. Norfolk footpaths are, like everything else here, a little eccentric and sometimes you will find it easier to walk alongside the path than actually on it. Apart from the King's Lynn and Norwich walks, which can be done in ordinary footwear, I recommend boots, wellingtons or at least strong shoes. It doesn't rain as much in Norfolk as in other parts of the country, so hopefully your waterproof will stay unused. And, of course, there aren't any real hills to tire you out. Good walking!

Will Martin

King's Lynn
The Tudor Rose Hotel

MAP: OS LANDRANGER 132 (GR 617204) OR A STREET MAP OF KING'S LYNN

WALK 1

DISTANCE: 2 MILES

DIRECTIONS TO START: THE TUDOR ROSE IS IN THE CENTRE OF KING'S LYNN ON ST NICHOLAS STREET, JUST OFF TUESDAY MARKET PLACE. **PARKING:** THE PAY-AND-DISPLAY CHAPEL STREET CAR PARK IS DIRECTLY OPPOSITE THE PUB. SEVERAL OTHER CAR PARKS ARE AVAILABLE NEARBY.

Once the fourth largest port in the country, King's Lynn has a fascinating history still clearly visible in the many superb buildings packed into a relatively small area. Its seaborne trade may have dwindled, but the town is proud of its maritime heritage and has made a huge effort recently to present it more attractively. The North Sea Haven project is particularly impressive, and its refurbished South Quay promenade gives an excellent view down the unpicturesque but oddly compelling Great Ouse river as it heads, dead straight, for the Wash.

This walk takes in most of the old town as well as circling through an attractive parkland area. The King's Lynn Town Walk map (available from the tourist information centre) is strongly recommended for more detail of the many buildings only briefly mentioned here.

The Tudor Rose Hotel

This atmospheric timber-framed pub dates from 1485, though it is possible part of the rear of the building is 300 years older, when the Bishop had his Winter Palace by the river here. It was for many years a wool merchant's house and it was not until the 1970s that it became a pub/restaurant after a period of standing derelict. Its resident ghost is the Grey Lady, said to be a bride killed by the lover she had jilted and seen mainly in the upstairs restaurant, a heavily-beamed room with a strong period feel.

Downstairs the beamed and panelled – but not over-restored – front bar is comfortable and welcoming, while the larger back bar has old-style furniture and interesting objects scattered around, including a spinning wheel. Outside there is a pleasantly shaded courtyard.

On the regular menu and specials board there's a good choice of traditional and foreign-influenced dishes, including Glastonbury lamb in a rich mint sauce, pork loin Dijonnaise, fillet of salmon Balmoral in brandy, lobster and cream sauce, and homemade steak and kidney pie. Vegetarian dishes include ricotta cannelloni and Stilton and leek bake, and the range of filled homemade hoagies is especially popular. Food is not served on Sundays.

Regular beers in this freehouse are Bateman XB from Lincolnshire, Timothy Taylor Landlord bitter and Bass, with a guest such as Hop and Glory from Ash Vine. There's also draught Murphy's, Carlsberg, Stella and Tetley.

The Tudor Rose has 13 bedrooms, 11 of them ensuite. Telephone: 01553 762824.

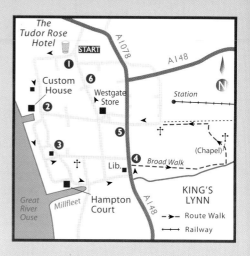

The Walk

① Turn right out of the pub into Tuesday Market Place, a handsome square where the centuries-old Lynn Mart fair starts every Valentine's Day. Head round to pass between the Globe and Woolpack hotels into King Street, with Lynn Arts Centre in the early 15th century Guildhall of St George on your right.

② Turn right on Purfleet Quay, where the 17th century Custom House has been beautifully restored as a tourist information centre/museum. Head to the end of the quay and a monument to famous travellers with Lynn connections, including the explorer George Vancouver, born here in 1757. Return to the Custom House, turn right and right again into King's Staithe Square. Now turn left onto South Quay and just before the Green Quay centre in the 1570 Marriott's Warehouse, turn left down College Lane with the Town Hall's chequered flintwork appearing ahead.

③ A short detour left through an ornate wooden door into the peaceful courtyard of

The 15th century Red Mount Chapel

stone gates turn left past the 15th century Red Mount Chapel. Turn left at the end and stay on the footpath, passing St John's church on your left.

⑤ At the road, cross and head down Blackfriars Street, with the Greyfriars Tower landmark over to your left. Continue into the pedestrian precinct, turn right by the Westgate store and follow the precinct round to the left.

⑥ At the end turn left and right into Chapel Street, past the 15th century Lattice House, now a pub. Turn left for the Tudor Rose, with on your right St Nicholas' Chapel and historic Pilot Street behind it well worth a look.

Thoresby College is recommended. Leaving the college, bear right into St Margaret's Place with St Margaret's church, founded in 1101, on your left. Note the unusual tide clock on the west tower. The 1475 Hanseatic Warehouse is on a lane to the right shortly. Continue ahead down Nelson Street, cross Church Street and walk down Millfleet to the carrstone library at the corner.

④ Cross the main road, going left, and turn right into Broad Walk, with its pleasant tree-lined pathways. Just before

PLACES OF INTEREST NEARBY

The **Green Quay** discovery centre, with saltwater aquaria and a variety of well-presented displays centred on the internationally important Wash estuary, is on the South Quay at King's Lynn. In an attractive old warehouse with a tearoom, it is open May to September 10 am to 6 pm; October to April 10 am to 4 pm. Telephone: 01553 818500.

True's Yard on North Street, King's Lynn, is a courtyard with the town's last remaining fishermen's cottages, restored to form a fascinating museum depicting this hard way of life. Open daily 9.30 am to 3.45 pm. Telephone: 01553 770479.

Wimbotsham
The Chequers

MAP: OS LANDRANGER 143
(GR 619052)

WALK 2

DISTANCE: 2¼ MILES

DIRECTIONS TO START: WIMBOTSHAM IS HALF A MILE OFF THE A10, JUST NORTH OF DOWNHAM MARKET. THE PUB IS IN THE CENTRE OF THE VILLAGE, OPPOSITE THE GREEN.
PARKING: IN THE PUB CAR PARK, WITH PERMISSION.

This stroll on quiet green lanes and well-defined paths takes you through the last corner of 'normal' countryside before the brooding expanse of West Norfolk fenland, the only hint of which is provided by the high embankment of the Great Ouse river. Wimbotsham is a village on an ancient site and has strong Norman connections – much of the land locally was held by William de Warenne, one of the Conqueror's most powerful subjects, as part of his huge estates in Norfolk, and St Mary's church with its two fine doorways dates from this period. The older parts of the village, featuring the rich browns of local carrstone, have an air of unchanging quietness, though this has not always been so. The village sign depicts a Wellington bomber, which was a familiar sight and sound flying from the nearby aerodrome in the Second World War.

The Chequers

This solid, brick-built village pub was extended at some stage in its history to take over an older carrstone cottage next door. It is a comfortable place with a friendly welcome, relying largely on local trade but also popular with holidaymakers and anglers.

The main bar has a wooden-floored area to the right where darts and dominoes are played, and to the left, passing a collection of wooden ducks, is the lounge/dining room hung with brasses. Up a few steps is a pleasant, wood-panelled non-smoking room doubling as a function room and featuring an interesting array of plates. Children and walkers are welcome, as are dogs in the bar area.

Food for the evening menu and lunchtime bar snacks is traditional in style with some foreign influence, and largely home-cooked using locally supplied ingredients. Popular dishes are moules marinières using mussels from Brancaster; beef, Guinness and mushroom cobbler; and surf 'n' turf – prawns on fillet steak. Roast chicken stuffed with pheasant stuffed with pork fillet is one of the more unusual dishes produced by the landlord/chef, and there is always a good vegetarian option, including such dishes as vegetable bourguignon with herb dumplings, and nut roast italienne. The Wimbo brunch and Wimbo BELT – an open bacon, egg, lettuce and tomato sandwich – are both popular lighter meals. Note: no food on Tuesday evenings.

Real ales in this Greene King house are IPA and Abbot, with occasional guests. Outside there is a sunny patio area. Telephone: 01366 387704.

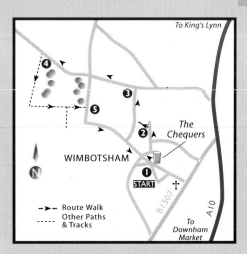

The Walk

① Turn right out of the pub and, after 50 yards, right on Tinker's Lane following a public path sign. Soon bear left on Miller's Lane, which becomes a track. Where this bends sharply right, follow a footpath straight ahead, with a Norfolk County Council circular walks waymarker. The path leads between hedges and, after 100 yards, you turn left over a stile, still with the NCC green arrow.

② Cross the field towards a group of sheds and climb a stile. Now keep to the left-hand edge of the field, which is used by a riding school. Go over another stile onto a path with the hedge on your left, then shortly over a fourth stile. Now turn right onto a lovely grassy track with fields on both sides and edged at intervals with elder bushes heavy with berries in season. Damselflies and several butterfly species are common here.

③ Continue to a crossroads of tracks and turn left. The broad green lane is lined now with more mature trees where a party of blue and coal tits busily searched for food as

Wimbotsham's attractive village sign

I passed. When you reach a road, cross and continue straight ahead on a gravel track with woodland on your left, following a fingerpost.

④ After 400 yards follow the main track when it bends round to the left shortly before a group of farm buildings that can be seen in the distance and continue alongside the wood. Over to the right the electric cables of the King's Lynn to London rail line can be seen and, beyond that, the embankment of the Great Ouse. Pass boarding kennels on your right and soon turn sharp left following the wood's edge. Pheasants scurry across your path as you keep straight ahead, ignoring a track to the right, to meet the road.

⑤ Now turn right and soon the lane bends sharply left into the village along Westway. There is a walkable verge on the right and then a pavement on the left as you pass some old carrstone houses and continue back to the pub.

PLACES OF INTEREST NEARBY

Welney Nature Reserve, run by the Wildfowl and Wetlands Trust, is famous for its spectacular numbers of visiting wild swans in winter but is well worth a visit at any time of year for its variety of wildlife. It has an excellent visitor centre with heated viewing gallery. South-west of Downham Market and signed off the A10, it is open daily except Christmas Day, 10 am to 5 pm. Swan feeding, floodlit after dusk, is daily from November to the end of February. Telephone: 01353 860711.

Snettisham
The Rose and Crown

MAP: OS LANDRANGER 132 (GR 686343)	**WALK 3**	**DISTANCE:** 1½ OR 3½ MILES

DIRECTIONS TO START: SNETTISHAM IS 10 MILES NORTH OF KING'S LYNN, ON THE OLD A149. FROM THE BYPASS HEAD INTO THE VILLAGE CENTRE AND TURN EASTWARDS ONTO OLD CHURCH ROAD. THE PUB IS ABOUT 100 YARDS ON THE LEFT. **PARKING:** IN THE LARGE CAR PARK BEHIND THE PUB.

Snettisham is an ancient village, famous for the discovery of spectacular hoards of gold torcs, or collars, and bracelets dating from the first century BC. Its distinctive character is created largely by the mellow brown carrstone quarried locally and of which most of the cottages are built. Nowadays it is equally well known among birdwatchers for the huge flocks of waders on the nature reserve fringing the Wash and geese that fly over the village in winter on their way to and from their feeding grounds. An unexpected cricketing connection is that W.G. Grace enjoyed holidays in the village in the early 1900s, staying with a headmaster friend, and the Rose and Crown's landlord is a cricket enthusiast too. Among the many items of interest on the pub walls is a bat given him by the doyen of commentators, E.W. Swanton.

The walk takes in the village centre as well as quiet paths and woodland skirting historic Ken Hill, with fine views to the Wash.

The Rose and Crown

Parts of this lovely whitewashed pub date back to the 14th century, its original purpose being to house workers building the village church. Its cosy interior is now an unusual and successful mix of old and new – a dining room extension in vibrant blues and yellows contrasting with the original beamed rooms with their tiled or wooden floors.

There's a friendly welcome for everyone ranging from village regulars to holidaymaking families with children, who will enjoy the walled garden with good (but unobtrusive) play equipment. In one bar there's an old 'penny seat' with a hole into which coins were tossed, a gambling game outlawed by George III but easily concealed, if the justices paid a call, by the simple method of sitting on it.

The Rose and Crown has an adventurous menu – 'pub food with a twist' is how they describe it – with such dishes as chargrilled halibut with carrot and cardamom puree, roast Mediterranean vegetables with basmati rice and saffron crème fraiche, and pan-fried pork fillet with Savoy cabbage and wild mushroom sauce. There is an à la carte evening menu and a daily specials blackboard that always includes a good range of vegetarian food.

This freehouse always has four or five real ales – Bass and Adnams Best Bitter are its regulars and there's also usually London Pride and Greene King IPA. Thirty wines are on the list, around a quarter available by the glass.

Accommodation is in 11 ensuite rooms in contemporary décor. Telephone: 01485 541382.

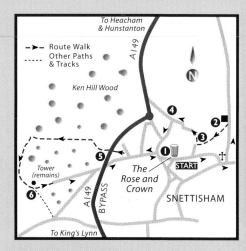

The Walk

① Turn left out of the pub to St Mary's church with its fine west window facing you. Go through the churchyard to the right corner, onto the lane and immediately left on a track with a fingerpost.

② After about 350 yards turn left just before a junction of tracks, through a metal gate, alongside farm outbuildings and left along the field edge. The path bends right at the bottom of the field, crossing a stile and through a gate. Now pass underneath a miniature railway track. Go through another gate and head diagonally right across two fields and then through a gate onto a broad track.

③ Turn right, uphill, through another gate and then left after recrossing the rail track. Go through a metal gate with buildings on your left, cross a field, through another gate and straight ahead on a track with carrstone houses on your left. Pass in front of the last house and along a narrow path between hedges, which then opens out into a field.

St Mary's church seen from across the meadows

④ At a broad track turn left to the main road. To complete a very short stroll, you could continue along the road to turn left again on Old Church Road, back to the pub. Otherwise, pass the Queen Victoria pub and turn right on Alma Road. Just after Cherry Tree Road, turn into a gravel track on the right, going immediately left through a metal gate and across the field towards a wood. Cross a plank bridge and go over a stile to the bypass, which you cross to a footpath sign.

⑤ Walk uphill through the lovely woodland of Ken Hill, ignoring all paths to right and left. Finally the path turns left along the edge of the wood with glimpses of the Wash through the trees. Where the path opens out with a good view across to the water, keep left on the wood edge.

⑥ Just after a metal gate, take the left fork and stay on this path until it meets a lane. Turn left to the bypass, go across and left again. After 50 yards turn right on Common Road East which heads back into the village. Turn right and then left on Old Church Road to the pub.

PLACES OF INTEREST NEARBY

Park Farm, Snettisham, is a family farmyard with a variety of 'gentle animals' which you can hand-feed and touch. It also runs safaris where you can feed a herd of deer. With craft shop and tearoom, it is open daily from 10 am to 5 pm. Telephone: 01485 542425.

Sandringham, just south of Snettisham, is the royal family's beautiful country residence with attractive gardens. The house, gardens and museum are open mid-April to mid-July and early August to early October, 11 am to 4.45 pm. Check the exact dates by telephoning 01553 772675.

Ringstead
The Gin Trap Inn

MAP: OS LANDRANGER 132 (GR 708403)   **WALK 4**   **DISTANCE:** 1½ OR 3¼ MILES

DIRECTIONS TO START: RINGSTEAD IS 3 MILES EAST OF HUNSTANTON. TURN EASTWARDS OFF THE A149 JUST NORTH OF HEACHAM AND THE PUB IS ON THE RIGHT OF THE MAIN STREET. **PARKING:** THE LANDLORD PREFERS YOU TO PARK IN THE LARGE VILLAGE HALL CAR PARK JUST BEFORE THE PUB.

(Photo courtesy of the Gin Trap Inn)

As the 50 mile long Peddars Way nears its destination on the North Norfolk coast, it takes to the high ground and offers a wonderful sense of openness and freedom. It is not hard, on this broad trail, to visualise one of the Roman soldiers for whom the route was built striding past you towards his goal. This walk perfectly captures the free spirit of the Peddars with the sky, such an essential ingredient of the Norfolk landscape, seeming even more enormous here than usual. But there is also much to appreciate in the way of wildlife and farming interest on the chalky soil, and Ringstead itself is a pretty carrstone village with a history stretching back, in fact, long before the Romans. Since there is little shade, this is a walk not best suited to young children on a hot day.

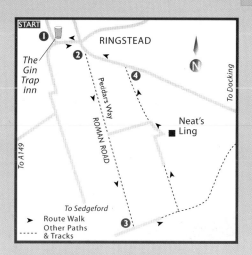

The Gin Trap Inn

The history of this popular pub is a tale of two names. Built in 1665 as a farmhouse, it became a coaching inn shortly afterwards called the Compasses. However, it fell derelict and when it reopened in 1972 there was already a pub of that name in nearby Snettisham. The Gin Trap was chosen for its farming (and alcoholic) connections and it is believed to be the only one in Britain. A large collection of traps now hang from the walls but they have not deterred the two resident ghosts – an elderly chap called Basil, who can sometimes be seen in his old seat in the corner, and an unnamed man from an earlier period wearing a coaching dustcoat.

The pub offers a range of traditional homemade food, and a daily specials board often features fresh local fish such as sea bass and also local crab. A Norfolk pie of pork with sage and onion is a speciality, and there are always four or five vegetarian options. Booking is advised for Saturday and Sunday evenings.

Apart from the beamed bar on two levels, there is a non-smoking dining room notable for a collection of 106 decorated chamber pots hanging from the ceiling. Real ales in this freehouse include Gin Trap Bitter, brewed by Woodforde's, the dark Norfolk Nog from the same brewery, plus Greene King Abbot and Adnams Best.

Outside there is a good-sized beer garden and a two-bedroom self-catering cottage converted from the old brew house. Telephone: 01485 525264.

The Walk

① Turn left out of the car park and left on the road signed to Docking. The road bends right, past a huge horse chestnut tree and, shortly, the Peddars Way branches off to the right, clearly signed.

② This broad track leads steadily uphill, past houses at first and then into open, rolling country with fine views on both sides. Where the soil is unplanted, you will see countless flints strewn on the surface – Ringstead is well known for the huge numbers of ancient flint tools found in the area over the years. There is now an opportunity to shorten the walk by taking the first broad track to the left, which leads down a point reached later on the main walk, close to Neat's Ling. Otherwise, keep straight ahead on a gently rising path that makes you feel like striding out back to the start of the Peddars Way at Knettishall Heath. After ¾ mile the track levels and becomes a narrower path along a field edge with a hedge on the right and then, after an acorn waymarker, with the hedge on your left. Skylarks sing in the vast expanse of sky and several butterfly species

The Peddars Way path leading down into Ringstead

flit in season along the grassy track by your feet.

③ At a T-junction turn left on a broad track and then, after about 200 yards, left again on a path signed 'Ringstead Rides' with a Norfolk County Council blue waymarker bearing a horse's head picture. The path heads uphill with pleasant views over to wooded country on the right and then turns right and left in front of farm buildings at Neat's Ling, built in carrstone with pantiled roofs. Ignore the track coming in from the left and keep straight ahead. In summer the path is now fringed with poppies and white campion, lapwings can be seen in tumbling flight and hares dash through the barley fields, often only their long ears showing above the crop.

④ At the road turn left and keep straight ahead, retracing your steps from the point where the Peddars Way comes in from the left, past the chestnut tree, back to the pub.

PLACES OF INTEREST NEARBY

Hunstanton is a pleasant seaside resort with a good beach and a variety of entertainment. The **Sea Life Centre** is family-orientated with hands-on exhibits and offers excellent underwater views of a wide range of sea creatures, including sharks and rays. Open daily except Christmas Day. Telephone: 01485 533576.

Norfolk Lavender at Heacham, in a lovely setting by the main coast road, shows how the herb is grown, harvested and processed, with trips to the lavender fields in season. Open daily except Christmas Day, Boxing Day and New Year's Day, 10 am to 5 pm. Telephone: 01485 570384. The nearby Heacham village sign features native American princess Pocahontas, who married tobacco planter John Rolfe, from an old Heacham family, in 1614 and came to England with him.

Brancaster
The Ship

MAP: OS LANDRANGER 132 (GR 773439)	**WALK 5**	**DISTANCE:** 3½ MILES

DIRECTIONS TO START: BRANCASTER IS ON THE A149 COAST ROAD 7 MILES EAST OF HUNSTANTON. THE PUB IS ON THE MAIN STREET AT THE HUNSTANTON END OF THE VILLAGE. **PARKING:** IN THE PUB CAR PARK, WITH PERMISSION.

Brancaster, once a Roman settlement with a strategic fort designed to repel Saxon raiders, is an attractive village on a beautiful stretch of North Norfolk coastline. Boats, birds and a bit of history dominate this walk which takes you up to the (relative) heights of Barrow Common, from where there are fine views down to the sea. From here you descend into the boaty world of Brancaster Staithe where the tidal creeks are full of small craft, ranging from smart weekend dinghies to fishing tubs that have seen many better days. Now there is a lovely stretch along the edge of the wide-open saltmarsh on the long-distance Norfolk Coast Path, which starts where the Peddars Way meets the sea at Holme and runs to Cromer. The site of Branodunum fort is right next to the path and though no building now remains, it is a place rich in atmosphere.

The Ship

In a nautical part of the world, this mid-18th century inn boasts not only a ship on its sign, but a large model of one on its end wall. The 6 ft long replica of an unnamed ship from the Nelson era is thought to be at least 100 years old and was bought 50 years ago at a London market by a family who had a seaside home at Brancaster.

There is something of the feel of a ship inside this friendly, comfortable pub too, with its wood-panelled bar and (non-smoking) dining room. Not far from the heart of Nelson territory, it also has a ghost called the White Lady, said to be the Admiral's childhood nanny who lived here at one time.

The Ship aims to serve good, traditional pub grub with a regular menu specialising in steaks and fish, and a daily specials board that takes in a wider range, including salmon in puff pastry with a lemon and asparagus sauce and peppered pork. There is always a choice of vegetarian food, including such dishes as broccoli and Brie rosti. Food is served from 12 noon to 2.30 pm and 6.30 pm to 9 pm (6 pm to 9 pm from July to mid-September, when the pub is open all day).

Regular real ales are Greene King IPA and Abbot, and also on draught are Boddingtons, Whitbread Best Mild, Stella, Guinness and Dry Blackthorn cider.

There is a pleasant beer garden, and the Ship offers accommodation in four bedrooms, two of them ensuite. Telephone: 01485 210333.

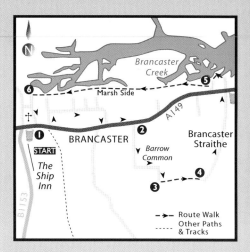

The Walk

① Turn right out of the pub and then left into Marsh Side, just before the garage. The quiet lane bends to the right and after 400 yards right again to meet the main coast road. Now cross and turn left to walk on a path by the roadside for 300 yards.

② Turn right on a broad, unsigned track which has a large tree trunk across it to stop cars. This leads gradually uphill between hedges full of elderflowers and wild roses in season. At the top of the slope there is a lovely view back over the marshes to the sea. The track bends left and, after 250 yards, right to become a narrower, grassy path.

③ Go through a metal gate and immediately turn left on a narrow path where there is a Barrow Common sign. This pleasant, shady path leads along the edge of a wood with more excellent views to the coast. Eventually it turns right out of the wood by an old concrete building and into open heathland before turning left to meet a lane.

Brancaster Creek

④ Now turn left and follow the lane downhill with Brancaster Staithe and the sea stretched out before you. Cross the main road by the Jolly Sailors pub and go straight ahead down a track. After 100 yards turn left, following yellow long-distance path signs, into a world of small boats.

⑤ Turn left after 100 yards at the main slipway road and almost immediately right on a narrow path between a building and parked boats. Turn left and right, following signs, and then keep straight ahead on the boardwalk by the marsh edge, where the calls of wading birds will accompany you, or even a drifting marsh harrier if you are lucky. After about a mile the site of Branodunum fort is on your left. Now pass several attractive flint cottages, ignore the first footpath sign and gate to the left and after 200 yards turn left by an Anglian Water building.

⑥ Keep straight ahead into London Street and turn right at the main road to the pub.

PLACES OF INTEREST NEARBY

Titchwell Marsh, just west of Brancaster, is one of the RSPB's most popular bird reserves, with a pleasant walk down to the beach and several hides. The reserve itself is open at all times and the visitor centre and well-stocked shop daily from 10 am to 5 pm April to October and 10 am to 4 pm November to March, except Christmas Day and Boxing Day. Telephone: 01485 210432.

West Rudham
The Duke's Head

MAP: OS LANDRANGER 132 (GR 815281)   **WALK 6**   **DISTANCE:** 3¼ MILES

DIRECTIONS TO START: WEST RUDHAM IS 7 MILES WEST OF FAKENHAM, ON THE A148. FROM THIS DIRECTION, THE DUKE'S HEAD IS ON THE RIGHT OF THE ROAD IN THE VILLAGE CENTRE. **PARKING:** IN THE PUB CAR PARK, WITH PERMISSION.

Farming has been the driving force here for centuries, right back to the Neolithic settlement that left its long barrow on West Rudham Common, where many rough tools and worked flints have been found. Much of the land locally was owned for years by the influential Townshend family, including Charles 'Turnip' Townshend, the politician and agricultural reformer who introduced the new vegetable from Holland in 1730 as a means of feeding cattle through the winter.

The other major local landowner was the Houghton estate, and this walk gives a brief view of the magnificent Palladian mansion of Houghton Hall, built by England's first prime minister, Sir Robert Walpole, in 1735. It also takes in farmland rich in wildlife and circles back through East Rudham – the names are derived from an Anglo-Saxon chieftain named Rudda – an attractive village despite being split by the busy A148 with its holiday traffic.

The Duke's Head

There is some doubt about when this attractive, friendly pub was built despite the date 1663 picked out in large numerals on the brickwork. This is probably when it was extended upwards, and the original building could be 100 years older. There is a mystery, too, about the letters HK by the date; the landlord jokily suggests Houghton Kennels, since it was once part of the nearby Houghton estate, but research continues. What is certain is that manorial court sessions were held at the inn for many years.

Inside there is a range of cosy, beamed rooms featuring two large brick fireplaces lit in winter. The bar area leads to two non-smoking dining rooms, including a cheerful family room, and one for smokers. Food on the main menu and daily specials board is described as 'modern English' and there is a strong local element, with such dishes as Norfolk gourmet sausages served with herb mash and Norfolk steak and ale pie. Fish is well represented, with smoked haddock and crab gratin and halibut steak just two of the offerings, and there are always vegetarian options. Puddings include the house speciality Norfolk Nudge, invented by the chef, which is a steamed sponge stuffed with bananas and cherries.

Real ales come from Woodforde's brewery – Wherry bitter, Nelson's Revenge and one other such as Kett's Rebellion. You will also find Boddingtons, draught Guinness, Heineken and Strongbow.

Outside there is pleasant trellised terrace. The Duke's Head is closed on Tuesdays. Telephone: 01485 528540.

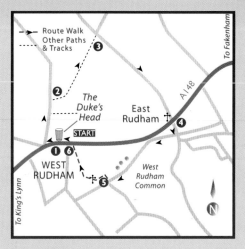

The Walk

① Turn right out of the pub and after 100 yards right again, following a public path sign up a broad sandy track. This soon gives lovely views of rolling farmland to the left, with Houghton Hall in the distance. Ignore the first broad track to the right.

② Opposite a wide gap in the hedge on the left, turn right on a narrower, grassy track favoured by butterflies in summer, including red admiral and clouded yellow. There is a good view back down to West Rudham as the track bends left between hedges before opening out into a meadow studded with wildflowers in season.

③ Turn right at the lane, heading downhill towards East Rudham, and at the main road turn right past the Cat and Fiddle. St Mary's church (key from post office) has an unusual octofoil window said to have been given by crusader knight Sir Aylmer de Mordaunt, who was saved from a shipwreck in 1290.

④ Cross the A148 and go down Station Road, after 50 yards turning right into a

Looking back to West Rudham

lane that runs alongside the green and then left into School Road. Opposite the playing field, next to a 30 mph sign, there is gap in the hedge where a short detour right takes you onto peaceful West Rudham Common, where the springy turf makes an ideal spot for a few minutes' rest. Unfortunately a footpath marked on the OS map does not lead across the common as it should, so return to the lane to continue for a further 100 yards.

⑤ Turn right over a stile between tall fir trees. Turn left on a 'conservation walk' along the field edge, which bends right and left to the 13th century St Peter's church, now redundant and maintained by Norfolk Churches Trust. Behind the church turn right along the right-hand field edge; the path is not clearly marked but heads along a broad, unploughed strip, with the hedge on your right.

⑥ Turn left at the field's end then right, heading for a white house and a footpath sign. Turn left across the village green to the pub.

PLACES OF INTEREST NEARBY

Bircham Windmill, north-west of Rudham and signed from Great Bircham village, is one of the best examples of a working mill in the country, with fine views from the top. There is a bakery using the mill's flour, a tearoom and cycle hire. It is open from Easter to the end of September. Telephone: 01485 578393.

Houghton Hall and gardens, with its herd of rare white deer, is approached by a minor road off the A148. Apart from the splendid rooms with fine furniture and paintings, there is a collection of 20,000 model soldiers. It is open Sundays, Thursdays and Bank Holiday Mondays from the beginning of April to near the end of September – check the exact dates and times by phoning 01485 528569.

Castle Acre
The Ostrich Inn

DIRECTIONS TO START: CASTLE ACRE IS 4 MILES NORTH OF SWAFFHAM, JUST LEFT OF THE A1065, TRAVELLING TOWARDS FAKENHAM. THE OSTRICH IS IN THE CENTRE OF THE VILLAGE, BY THE GREEN. **PARKING:** IN THE PUB CAR PARK, THROUGH THE ARCHWAY TO THE LEFT OF THE BUILDING.

In its ancient hilltop setting above the gently flowing River Nar, Castle Acre is one of Norfolk's most attractive villages, whose centre still has a timeless quality to it. Its key position as a river crossing point on the Peddars Way dates back to Roman times, and the picturesque ruins of its Cluniac priory and castle show its later importance as both an ecclesiastical and military stronghold.

The walk starts in the village centre, which has several specialist shops, and then takes in green lanes and paths on both sides of the river. It also touches on a large area of pleasant sheep meadow opened up to the public under a countryside access scheme. A distant view of the recently built wind turbine at Swaffham – the tallest in the country – seems appropriate as a new slant on ancient technology.

The Ostrich Inn

This 16th century coaching inn is one of several pubs in the area with the same unusual name. The explanation is not – as some might argue – that the ostrich's head-in-sand reputation mirrors the typical Norfolkman's view of the world outside, but that they were all on the estates of the Earl of Leicester, whose seat is Holkham Hall, near Wells, and on whose coat of arms the bird appears.

The Ostrich has a homely atmosphere with beamed rooms and a big log fire on cold days, and the landlord has long specialised in pub food. He now offers a varied choice with a strong international flavour – he swaps recipes with chefs around the world via the internet. Among the exotic meats regularly on the menu is, you guessed it, ostrich, but also emu, bison, kangaroo and crocodile.

Dishes on the specials board could include Jamaican jerky butterfly chicken, Cajun grilled golden trout and smoked sausage and sauerkraut. There's also an unusually good vegetarian selection, including such dishes as aromatic chickpeas with basmati rice, and spinach, cheese and nut pie. Puddings too have an international flavour, with baclava and galatabourica alongside spotted dick and treacle roly poly.

The pub is tied to Greene King and offers its range of IPA bitter, Abbot strong ale and XX dark mild.

Children are welcome in a high-ceilinged room which also offers display space to local artists, and there is a pleasant beer garden with an aviary and rabbits. The pub has B&B accommodation. Telephone: 01760 755398.

The Walk

① Turn left out of the pub and right through the 13th century Bailey Gate. Turn left just before the Methodist church to the castle, founded soon after the Norman Conquest of 1066. It now stands in ruins but the the earthworks are among Britain's most impressive. There is a fine view over the Nar to Swaffham, with its wind turbine on the skyline. Skirt the castle, crossing a wooden bridge, up steps and turning right down steps. Just before a road, climb a stile to the right following a footpath fingerpost. Pass a row of cottages on the left, go over a stile and follow the path round to the left and another stile.

② At the road turn right and after 200 yards left into a lane, following byroad and Nar Valley Way signs. The road becomes a track heading straight uphill; at a fork, bear right, over a stile and between overhanging hedges.

③ Turn right when the path meets a lane and, shortly, at Newton Mill, go over the bridge and immediately left on a track to the main road.

④ Cross the busy A1065 and turn sharp right on the 'dead' bed of the old road.

PLACES OF INTEREST NEARBY

The **EcoTech** environmental discovery centre close to the Safeway store in Swaffham has the UK's tallest wind turbine (300 ft) with a viewing platform and tells the story of the earth's evolution, climate and peoples. A good place for children, with interactive displays, it also has an organic garden. It is open round the year, Monday to Friday 10 am to 4 pm, last admission 3 pm. For details of the viewing platform, telephone 01760 726100.

The castle ruins

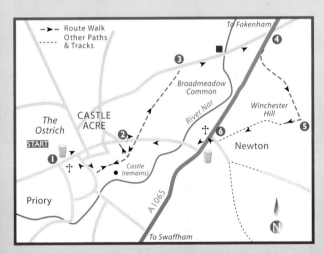

⑤ Turn right, still following a footpath sign, up Winchester Hill with pleasant views over the valley. Follow the track downhill, passing Manor House on the right, and turn right at a lane to the main road.

⑥ Turn left past the George and Dragon and right after 100 yards down a lane signed 'Castle Acre'. Cross the Nar and where the byroad turns right, go left over a stile into 'open access' land. There is no clearly defined path but head diagonally uphill across the meadow and then retrace your steps back to the castle and pub.

Earth has been piled in a gateway to keep out cars, but walk round it and ahead for 200 yards. Turn left on a track which soon bends left and right then ahead through a gate, following a yellow arrow. After 300 yards pass through a gap in a tall hedge.

Cockley Cley
The Twenty Churchwardens

MAP: OS LANDRANGER 144 (GR 792043) **WALK 8** **DISTANCE:** 2¼ MILES

DIRECTIONS TO START: COCKLEY CLEY IS 4 MILES SOUTH-WEST OF SWAFFHAM, REACHED BY MINOR ROADS OFF THE A1065. THE PUB IS IN THE VILLAGE CENTRE, NEXT TO THE CHURCH. **PARKING:** IN THE PUB CAR PARK.

Breckland is one of the most distinctive and, from both a historic and wildlife point of view, interesting areas of Norfolk. Once one of the strongholds of Queen Boudicca's Iceni tribes – Cockley Cley itself had a settlement where now a replica village-museum stands – for centuries it was semi-desert, its sandy ground covered in expanses of dry heathland. This was the 'broken land' that gave the name 'breck' to the area and for many years its main product was rabbits, introduced and kept in enormous warrens that still feature in the local place names. Extensive planting of pines from the end of the 18th century changed things dramatically, providing windbreaks against the drifting sand and allowing cultivation to take place. There are still small areas of ancient heathland, though the dark forests with their broad 'rides' through the trees now dominate the countryside.

This walk starts in an ancient and peaceful village and goes on to give a flavour of the sharp contrast between forest and open landscape.

The Twenty Churchwardens

This is an old-style convivial pub with a unique name and a diverse history including use as a church and polling station. It was not until 1968 that it came into being, after the village had been publess for a couple of years. Landowner Sir Peter Roberts decided to remedy the situation and created the pub from the old schoolhouse and a couple of cottages attached to it.

All that was missing was the name, and it was the rector who, bearing in mind the village had just become the tenth to join the local group of parishes, each with two churchwardens, figured it out.

Inside there is no piped music or fruit machine – the landlady believes in the value of lively conversation – and the walls are crammed with old village photographs and other memorabilia, including the school bell and a fan-shaped display of 20 churchwarden pipes.

The style of food is simple 'but not boring' home-cooked dishes with the speciality a range of flans including Swiss onion; chicken and (locally grown) asparagus; steak and mushroom; and spinach and ricotta. A reflection, perhaps, of the house sense of humour is the Heart Attack Sandwich, of sausage, bacon, egg, potato waffle, mushroom and tomato, described as a 'deadly filling'. Booking is advised for the Sunday roast lunch; there is no food on Sunday evenings.

This freehouse has Adnams Best Bitter, plus one or two other real ales from local breweries. There is a pleasant patio area. Telephone: 01760 721439.

The Walk

① Turn left out of the pub and up Pine Avenue, which is also signed 'Peddars Way Bridle Route'. This is a quiet lane lined with tall pines and passes houses on the right before opening out with views through trees on both sides. There are often good numbers of birds here – goldfinches feeding on seed heads along the field edge, coal tits and long-tailed tits in the trees.

② After about 500 yards bear right off the lane along a grassy track, following a Peddars Way fingerpost and blue arrow. Keep straight ahead, with large open fields on the left, passing an old flint barn. In summer, butterflies are common on this pleasant track, whose grassy edges are dotted with blue speedwell and bright yellow gorse.

③ Soon the track forks left into conifer woodland, still following the bridle route sign. Logging is carried out by Forest Enterprise in this area, and there may be warnings to keep to the paths. Where the main track bends right and a smaller one comes in from the left, keep straight ahead,

The village green

following the blue arrow on a narrow path between trees, into a stretch of broadleaved woodland then more conifers.

④ When you reach a clearing, ignore the path straight ahead with the blue arrow and turn left on a much broader track which takes you through a stretch of tall, slender conifers with an atmosphere of cathedral-like calm. The track now passes through an area of new planting where there is a reasonable chance of seeing woodlarks. Slightly smaller than skylarks, with more prominent white eyestripes and a much shorter tail, they are among our rarest breeding birds but are doing particularly well in Breckland.

⑤ When the track meets the lane, turn left and head back to the pub. There are glimpses of gorse-dotted heathland

through trees to the right before cultivated fields of typical Breckland light, sandy soil on both sides. Back in Cockley Cley, All Saints' church with its probable Saxon origins and remains of a round tower which collapsed in 1991 is well worth a look.

PLACES OF INTEREST NEARBY

Cockley Cley Iceni Village and Museums, close to the Twenty Churchwardens, is a reconstruction of the type of village believed to have been on this site, occupied by Queen Boudicca's Iceni tribespeople shortly before the Roman occupation. There is also a museum of East Anglian life in an Elizabethan cottage, probably the oldest Saxon church in the country (AD 630) and a nature trail. Open April to October daily 11 am to 5.30 pm, except July and August when the hours are 10 am to 5.30 pm. Telephone: 01760 721339 or 724588.

Mundford
The Crown Hotel

MAP: OS LANDRANGER 144 (GR 803938) | **WALK 9** | **DISTANCE:** 3¾ MILES

DIRECTIONS TO START: MUNDFORD IS 8 MILES NORTH OF THETFORD AT THE JUNCTION OF THE A1065 AND A134. THE PUB IS IN THE VILLAGE CENTRE DOWN CROWN ROAD, OFF THE MAIN ROAD JUST ON THE SWAFFHAM SIDE OF THE JUNCTION. **PARKING:** THERE IS LIMITED PARKING AT THE PUB, WITH PERMISSION, OR ROUND THE VILLAGE GREEN.

Trees are the focal point of this walk, ranging from the conifer plantations of Thetford Forest – not to everyone's taste but with a character all their own – to the beautiful specimen trees of Lynford Arboretum and finally a broad walk lined with a double row of magnificent giant redwoods. The arboretum was first planted just over 50 years ago among the mature trees of Lynford Hall woodland and makes an attractive visit in its own right. The walk also takes in a lakeside path with picturesque views of the hall, a hidden church and unusual wildlife, including a good chance of crossbills in the arboretum, possible red squirrels and probable muntjac deer, an introduced species now increasing dramatically in Norfolk, much to the concern of naturalists. Mundford itself is an attractive village that maintains its quiet atmosphere despite being close to the junction of two busy roads.

The Crown Hotel

This pub prides itself on an informal style of 'old-fashioned hospitality' and has long played a central role in village life. Built in 1652, it became a well-known hunting inn serving the nearby Lynford estate – the 'Squire of All England' George Osbaldeston was a guest during a shoot in which the bag included 309 pheasant. Later a magistrates' court was held here and much later still its Old Court Restaurant was used as a doctor's surgery where, it is said, the sound insulation was so poor you could clearly discover the ailments of the other patients while you were waiting.

Nowadays the Crown has a range of cosy beamed bars and dining rooms where the food is imaginative and attractively presented using locally grown ingredients where possible. The bar menu has such dishes as chicken jalfrezi, local trout, Crown Dinner Jacket – a baked potato stuffed with mushrooms, spring onions and mozarella cheese – and local herb sausage. The à la carte menu offers, among other delights, a medley of local duck, and baked monkfish with lobster tails. There is a daily specials board that always includes a good choice of fish and vegetarian dishes.

Regular real ales are Marston's Pedigree and Courage Directors plus, usually, Woodforde's Wherry bitter and guests from the Iceni Brewery just up the road at Ickburgh.

Children are made welcome both in the pub and outside in the walled beer garden, and the hotel has accommodation in a dozen ensuite rooms. Telephone: 01842 878233.

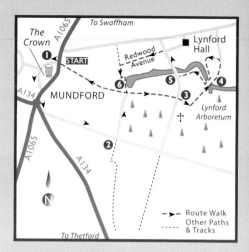

The Walk

① Turn left out of the pub and at the main road bear right to the roundabout. Turn left and after 100 yards left again on a lane, following a sign for Lynford Lakes.

② After ½ mile turn left down a track into the forest, following a black arrow on a yellow background. Immediately before a house turn right, ignore a left turn and continue ahead down a broad, grassy track. Soon you cross a main track (ignore a path to the left signed 'Lynford Lakes') but it is worth detouring to the Catholic church of Our Lady of Consolation. To do this, turn right at the main track and after 100 yards left down a path between trees to the tiny church, with its exquisite knapped flintwork.

③ Back at the crossing of tracks, continue on your route eastwards (turning right off the main track if you have detoured to the church) and after 100 yards turn sharp left by a large horse chestnut tree down a broad path. This crosses a bridge at the end of a lake for a loop round Lynford Arboretum, but note that dogs are not allowed.

Lynford Hall

④ Walk up the hill and turn left on a gravel path, past a four-pillared arch and follow the path as it curves back to the bridge. Recross the bridge and turn right on the path alongside the lake, where there is now a splendid view of Lynford Hall.

⑤ Turn right over a bridge at the end of the lake and carry on up the track. Opposite the hall gates, turn left by a sculpture of bulls in combat and head down a broad walk between rows of redwoods. At the bottom of this alley, turn left by a blue-topped stump. Ignore the left turn at the end of the lake, keep straight on for 50 yards and go through a black-and-yellow poled gate.

⑥ Turn right and take a path to the right of the cottage passed earlier, through a wood. Keep straight ahead on a grassy track through fields and over a stile just before the main road. Cross and walk down a gravelled lane back to the pub.

PLACES OF INTEREST NEARBY

Grime's Graves are prehistoric flint mines, said to be the oldest major industrial site in Europe, where you can descend one of the excavated shafts and see how Stone Age man produced a range of beautiful flint tools. The site is signed off the A134 south-east of Mundford and is open from 1 April to 30 September 10 am to 6 pm; 1 to 31 October 10 am to 5 pm; November to the end of March, Wednesdays to Sundays, 10 am to 4 pm. Telephone: 01842 810656.

The Ancient House Museum at Thetford is in a fine 15th century timber-framed house and includes displays on the Thetford treasure of Roman jewellery and on local man Thomas Paine, whose *Rights of Man* was a key influence on revolutionary France and America. Telephone 01842 752599 for opening times.

Burnham Thorpe
The Lord Nelson

MAP: OS LANDRANGER 132 (GR 852416)   WALK 10   DISTANCE: 3¼ MILES

DIRECTIONS TO START: BURNHAM THORPE IS REACHED BY MINOR ROADS EAST OF THE B1355 BETWEEN BURNHAM MARKET AND NORTH CREAKE. THE PUB IS IN THE VILLAGE CENTRE. **PARKING:** IN THE PUB CAR PARK, WITH PERMISSION.

This lovely flint and pantiled village has, thankfully, resisted the temptation to become a Nelson Experience theme park in honour of our hero of Trafalgar. A plaque on a wall a mile away marks Horatio's birthplace in the now demolished Parsonage, the church has a well-presented display on his life and the pub has a couple of unostentatious groups of memorabilia, relying mainly on preserving an atmosphere of history. But 'dear, dear Burnham', as Nelson described it, is still the peaceful backwater it always was.

This walk takes in the village, with meadowland and stream along its length, and also visits All Saints' church, which is well worth a visit in its own right, even apart from the Nelson connection. It also heads out into typical North Norfolk farmland with its big skies and feeling of airy openness.

The Lord Nelson

If Horatio could revisit his local today, virtually the only surprises would be his own memorabilia on the walls – and the name of the hostelry itself. When he held a leaving party in 1793 at the Plough, as it then was, before taking command of the 64-gun *Agamemnon*, his greatest triumphs lay ahead.

But the 1650s building has scarcely changed: small rooms with high-backed wooden settles, flagstone and brick floors, even the method of serving drinks is the same. For this is one of very few pubs in Britain with no bar – beer is drawn from casks in a back stillroom. You choose your table and one of the friendly staff soon appears to take your order.

The food might strike Nelson as slightly unusual, despite his foreign travels, for besides the gammon and sirloin steaks, the specials board shows a modern and Mediterranean touch. Sautéed chicken breast with strawberry salsa; roast rack of lamb with pear and mint; baked tart of broccoli, olives and sun-dried tomatoes are among the offerings. In winter food is served only five days a week – check first.

The real ales include, fittingly, Nelson's Revenge from Woodforde's, and Kett's Rebellion is a frequent guest. Greene King Abbot and IPA are regulars. The drinks blackboard also offers Nelson's Blood, a rum and spice mixture described by the landlady as 'horrible' but apparently popular.

While inside there is the snuggest snug imaginable, outside there is a large, attractive beer garden with good play equipment. Telephone: 01328 738241.

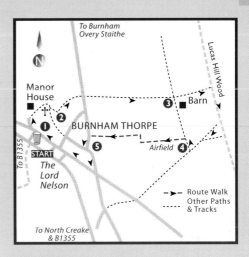

The Walk

① Turn left out of the pub and, after 50 yards, turn right on a lane alongside the clear stream (actually the somewhat ambitiously named River Burn) heading for the church. Pass the Manor House on the left and as the lane bends right to the church, bear left up a broad track. All Saints' church with its splendid chequered flintwork is where Nelson's father Edmund was Rector and where Nelson himself fully expected to be buried, before his fame made Westminster Abbey a more fitting resting place.

② The track curves left uphill, giving good views back down to Burnham Thorpe, before crossing a lane and heading for a red-roofed barn in the distance. This is good, open agricultural land, with rippling fields of barley and where the soil also suits vegetables such as potatoes and parsnips.

③ At the barn keep straight on, heading for Lucas Hill Wood, and then turn right alongside the wall of the Holkham Park estate. Follow this shady path between the

Horatio Nelson is proudly displayed on the village sign

left now there is, indeed, a grassy landing strip used by private light aircraft. After about 200 yards and just after another airstrip sign facing in the opposite direction, turn left on a grassy track between trees. The vegetation, including nettles, can be thick here but it is not a long stretch. Go through a gap in the hedge and along the field edge with a hedge on your right. At the bottom of the field turn right and immediately left along another field.

⑤ At the lane, turn left and follow it round to a T-junction. Turn right along the main village street, past attractive flint cottages by the river and the village sign featuring Nelson, back to the pub.

wall and a hedge until it bends right after 300 yards, away from the wall through trees at first and then into open fields.

④ At a junction of paths turn right where there is an 'Active Airstrip' sign. To your

PLACES OF INTEREST NEARBY

Holkham Hall is the classic 18th century Palladian-style mansion of the Coke family, Earls of Leicester, situated in splendid grounds with a deer park. It offers lakeside walks, a walled garden, a museum, pottery and an excellent art collection. The hall is open from the beginning of June to the end of September, Sunday to Thursday. Telephone 01328 710227 for exact times.

Thompson
The Chequers

| **MAP:** OS LANDRANGER 144 (GR 922969) | **WALK 11** | **DISTANCE:** 3 MILES |

DIRECTIONS TO START: THOMPSON IS ABOUT 4 MILES SOUTH OF WATTON, OFF THE A1075. THE PUB IS JUST NORTH OF THE VILLAGE CENTRE. **PARKING:** IN THE PUB CAR PARK, WITH PERMISSION.

This walk starts in typical open Norfolk farmland but then, in sharp contrast, plunges into the mysterious watery world of the pingo – no strange aquatic creature this, but a prehistoric creation nonetheless, making Thompson Common look like a set from Jurassic Park. Pingos are shallow, circular pools formed after lenses of frozen water pushed through the soil surface in the Ice Age. These hillocks later melted and collapsed into water-filled craters. Rare in the rest of Britain, having been mostly lost to agricultural drainage, here they are dotted about the damp common to form a habitat rich in wildlife. The oddly-named village itself, just east of the Peddars Way, was originally Tomestuna, from the Danish personal name Tumi and tun, a settlement. In the Middle Ages its church, St Martin's, had a college of priests attached to it and 'College' is still featured in several local place names.

The Chequers

This 16th century thatched inn is well known to walkers for its warm welcome and good food. Its beamed and low-ceilinged interior has two tiny central snugs and dining rooms on either side, the larger of which is non-smoking.

Besides being a pub, court sittings of the nearby Merton Hall were held here as early as 1724, dealing with rents, lettings of land and crimes against the manor. The pub sign shows a knight on his charger carrying a chequered shield, but this reflects a history of financial dealings rather than combat as a chequered cloth was commonly used for ease of counting out rent money – hence the word 'exchequer'.

There is a wide choice of food ranging from traditional steaks, grills and game such as pheasant and wild duck to occasional more exotic fare such as ostrich and kangaroo. Fish and vegetarian dishes are well represented and there is a separate children's menu. A daily specials board offers dishes such as venison steak with a strawberry and green peppercorn sauce, and puddings including toffee and apple meringue roulade.

Real ales are Adnams Best Bitter, Fuller's London Pride, Greene King IPA and Wolf from the independent brewery at nearby Attleborough, and there are regular guests. The wine list includes Elmham Park white from Norfolk.

Food is served lunchtimes and evenings seven days a week and booking is recommended. There is a beer garden with play area, and bed and breakfast is available in a newly built extension. Telephone: 01953 483360.

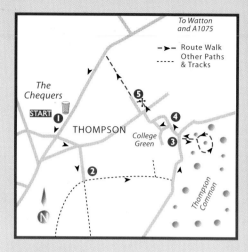

The Walk

① Turn right out of the pub and, at the crossroads, left on School Road. The village sign here shows a pilgrim, goose girl and Roman soldier on the ancient Peddars Way to the North Norfolk coast. Pass the school and, at a junction of roads, turn right on Hall Lane. Thompson's 'dead-end' nature is evident here in the 'no through road' signs – a huge military training area created during the Second World War, engulfing several villages, is nearby.

② After just over 200 yards, at a path junction, turn left following a blue bridleway arrow. The path heads through crops towards a thatched cottage to meet a lane, on which you turn left and continue as it bends through woodland.

③ Just before a junction, turn right on a footpath following a Great Eastern Pingo Trail arrow. The path bends left into damp woodland, across a stream and through a kissing gate. Thompson Common stretches ahead with a variety of birdlife, and you may see muntjac deer or even the small herd of Shetland ponies that roams wild

Shetland ponies on Thompson Common (photo courtesy of G. Bradshaw)

here. Turn right and the path now circles left before reaching an area dotted with pingos. Turn acutely left just before reaching a large pond on your right. This narrower, unsigned path bends left through light woodland to meet a wire fence. Turn left and, after 100 yards, go diagonally left between gorse bushes on a path back to the kissing gate. Retrace your steps to the lane, turn right then almost immediately bear left on a lane signposted 'Thompson'.

④ After 100 yards or so turn left on College Road and go over a bridge to the hamlet of College Green, with several picturesque cottages. Turn right at the T-junction and left at the next junction. The lane now leads to the fine 14th century St Martin's church, built of knapped flint with chequerwork at the base of the tower.

⑤ Walk through the churchyard to the left corner and come out on a footpath, where you turn right and head across fields to meet a lane. Turn left and walk the short distance back to the pub.

PLACES OF INTEREST NEARBY

East Wretham Heath nature reserve by the A1075 south of Thompson is run by Norfolk Wildlife Trust as traditional heathland grazed by sheep and rabbits. It offers attractive paths with a good variety of birds and plants, some ancient Scots pines and two lakes, Ringmere and Langmere, which mysteriously dry up at times. The reserve is open daily from 8 am to dusk and admission is free. Telephone: 01842 755010.

The Tropical Butterfly Garden and Bird Park at Great Ellingham, off the B1077 to Attleborough, has stunningly beautiful free-flying butterflies and a falconry centre. It is open daily 9 am to 5.30 pm, Sundays and bank holidays 10 am to 5.30 pm. Telephone: 01953 453175.

Swanton Morley
Darby's

DIRECTIONS TO START: SWANTON MORLEY IS 4 MILES NORTH-EAST OF EAST DEREHAM ON THE B1147. THE PUB STANDS AT A JUNCTION OF THREE ROADS IN THE CENTRE OF THE VILLAGE. **PARKING:** IN THE TOP CAR PARK OF THE PUB.

You cannot help but notice a strong military presence in Norfolk, and though the noise of low-flying jet fighters is sometimes a nuisance, there is a fascinating and often poignant side to the county's history of combat. This walk takes in a particularly moving reminder of the young men who were stationed at the airbase on the fringe of Swanton Morley and gave their lives during the Second World War. In a corner of the sloping churchyard, with views over a tranquil valley below, are rows of Servicemen's graves. Most were natives of Australia, Canada and New Zealand – several of them no more than 19 or 20 years old when they died so far from home. The RAF left the base fairly recently and it has now been taken over by the Army. The rest of this short walk takes you on green lanes and byroads amid typical Norfolk farmland scenery and back through the village.

Darby's

This is a cosy pub with a laid-back family atmosphere, a wide choice of food and real ale, and an unusual history. It was built in the late 1880s as a farmhouse for Ann Darby and became a pub only 13 years ago, having been divided into two cottages in the meantime.

The agricultural connection is still strong. Its owner runs two nearby farms one of which, Park Farm, has a caravan and camping site and eight guest rooms converted from barns. The walls of the beamed pub are hung with farming implements and the bar 'stools' are seats from a sprout-planting machine, whose current use is in pleasant contrast to the original back-aching labour.

The food is an interesting mixture of the traditional – scrumpy pork steak with cider and apple sauce, for example – and oriental, since the pub has a Thai chef cooking authentic dishes such as tiger prawns in oyster sauce with cashew nuts. There is also an especially good range of snacks.

Real ale regulars are Adnams Best Bitter and Broadside, Greene King IPA, Hall and Woodhouse Tanglefoot and Woodforde's Wherry. There are always two or three guests and also Boddingtons, Stella and a draught cider.

Children are welcome throughout the pub but usually prefer to be outside in the large beer garden with adventure playground equipment. Darby's is open all day Saturday and Sunday, and food is served seven days a week. There are regular special events such as a children's day over Easter. Telephone: 01362 637647.

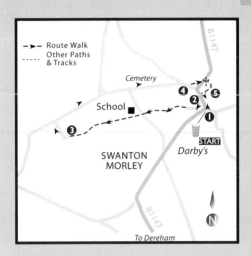

The Walk

① Cross the road outside the pub and walk up Town Street. After 50 yards, just before the village sign, turn left up a broad path to the Mill Bakery. Village signs are very much a feature of Norfolk, ranging from traditional scenes to a modern, almost sculpture-like style. Swanton Morley's is a fine painted sign showing the lord of the manor, Sir William de Morley, and his wife receiving rents in the 15th century. On top is a carving of the paper mill, reflecting the village's major industry in years gone by.

② Turn left in front of the bakery and follow the broad track round to the right. The path climbs gradually and crosses a lane, following a public bridleway sign. On the right is the village school, which has a large brightly-coloured painting on its end wall called 'Travel the World' reflecting the travels of its children, many of whom live on the Army base. Keep straight ahead between hedges to a T-junction of tracks.

③ Turn right. After 200 yards turn right on a lane, passing on your left a pair of cottages built of Norfolk 'softs', a lovely,

The delightful village sign at Swanton Morley

delightful view from the far end across the unspoilt valley of the River Wensum with a small round-towered church in the middle distance. In the bottom left corner of the churchyard are the Servicemen's graves.

⑤ Go down a path from the main church entrance, through a gate and turn right, past the bowling green and back to the road. The Paper Makers pub opposite also bears witness to the village's former industry. Now turn left and walk back down Town Street passing three brick cottages on your left, named Jack's Cottage, Edie's Cottage and Lottie's Cottage, to the pub.

mellow red brick. Keep straight ahead on the lane, ignoring a road to the left, and soon pass a small cemetery.

④ At a T-junction turn right with a pavement on the left side of the road. Bear left over Mill Street to the large, airy All Saints' church. Walk round the church for a

PLACES OF INTEREST NEARBY

Norfolk Rural Life Museum and Union Farm at Gressenhall, just west of Swanton Morley off the B1146, is in the unusual setting of a former Victorian workhouse. It has well-presented displays on village life and rural trades and a child-friendly farm worked by heavy horses, with several rare breeds of livestock. It is open from the beginning of April to the end of October, check the exact dates and times by telephoning 01362 860563.

Cley next the Sea
The George & Dragon Hotel

MAP: OS LANDRANGER 133 (GR 046439)   **WALK 13**   DISTANCE: 2½ MILES

DIRECTIONS TO START: CLEY IS ON THE A149 COAST ROAD 7 MILES WEST OF SHERINGHAM. THE PUB IS ON A SHARP BEND IN THE CENTRE OF THE VILLAGE. **PARKING:** IN THE CAR PARK BEHIND THE PUB, WITH PERMISSION.

This is a classic stroll into birdland, but even if winged things don't set your senses twitching there is so much more to enjoy in the expanse of marsh, sea and sky laid out before you. Until the early 17th century Cley Marsh was saltings covered by the sea at high tide, but in 1649 the lord of the manor embanked it to provide flood protection and improve the grazing. Countless nature-lovers have been grateful he did as this is now among Britain's premier birdwatching sites with an albatross-wing-length list of rarities.

Cley village itself was once a major port on the estuary of the River Glaven but this has long silted up and the 'next the Sea' part of its name is now a quirk of history. An attractive place nonetheless, with an interesting collection of specialist shops including a famous smokehouse, art gallery, pottery and delicatessen.

The George & Dragon Hotel

With a bird 'bible' of local sightings on a brass lectern in one bar and a residents' lounge called the Hide – complete with binoculars and view over a specially created lagoon – there is no mistaking where the George's main claim to fame lies. Its birdy ties go back to its late 19th century rebuilding, on a much earlier inn site, as a brewery flagship where the directors hosted shooting parties. In 1926 the Norfolk Naturalists Trust, from which all others have sprung, was founded here and there can hardly be a serious birder who has not had a pint at some time.

The George is a past winner of the CAMRA award for best pub food in Norfolk. It aims at an 'informal but efficient' style and has a wide choice using a high proportion of local ingredients, including the seashore plant samphire. Crab dishes are a speciality – crab features, along with prawns and Cley cider-pickled herring, in a Fantasy of Seafood – as is pan haggerty, a cheese, onion and potato bake served with bacon and sausages. A good choice of vegetarian dishes is always on offer.

Regular real ales are IPA and Abbot from Greene King, plus Morland Old Speckled Hen, with occasional guests. There is also an unusual collection of Calvados apple brandies, which you would probably have to go some distance into France to equal. A French touch, too, in the beer garden boules strip overlooking the marshes.

There is overnight accommodation in nine double rooms. Telephone: 01263 740652.

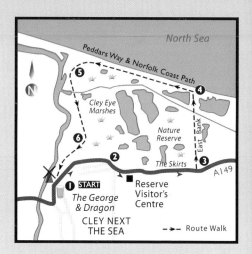

The Walk

① Turn right out of the pub and continue along the main street with Cley Mill, now a hotel, to your left. Soon there is a raised path on the right of the road with views over the marshes, where sedge warblers sing, oblivious to passing holiday traffic.

② Cross the road and then, just past a lane to the right signed 'Newgate', turn left onto a boardwalk running between the road and a dyke. The thatched Cley Marshes visitor centre across the road is worth visiting for views over the lagoons and information on current birds. The boardwalk becomes a grassy path leading into a small car park. Go up the bank and turn left on the raised path heading for the sea.

③ This is the East Bank, possibly Britain's best-known birdwatching spot, where celebrity visitors are almost as frequent as rare birds. With the ever-changing colours of rippling reedbeds to your left and grazing marsh stretching away to your right, this is a splendid path. Birds are everywhere, at all times of the year,

Cley Mill

including graceful avocets on the open water of Arnold's Marsh as the path nears the sea and the possibility of the more elusive bittern and bearded tit.

④ Go up the shingle bank and turn left on the ridge, part of the North Norfolk Coast Path, which lifts you up between the crashing waves and the marshes. Seabirds are now added to the reedbed warblers and waders, the elegance and power of a diving Sandwich tern one example of what could be on offer.

⑤ After about ⅔ mile of shingle walking – not something you can hurry over – turn left at the car park and beach café, a near-legendary birders' tea stop which also has public toilets. Take the raised path on the right of the road, heading inland.

⑥ After a while the path bends away from the road towards Cley Mill, one of Norfolk's most photographed buildings. It passes to the left of the mill, through a car park and back to the main road. Turn right to the pub.

PLACES OF INTEREST NEARBY

Cley Marshes reserve, run by Norfolk Wildlife Trust, is one of the premier birdwatching sites in the country with a huge list of resident and visiting species. The visitor centre, with shop and refreshments, offers the use of binoculars and telescope, and there are several thatched hides reached by paths through the reedbeds. The reserve is open all year round, but closed on Mondays except bank holidays. The centre is open from April to October 10 am to 5 pm; tickets for the reserve during winter are available from the warden at Watcher's Cottage 200 yards from the car park towards Cley. Telephone: 01263 740008.

Reepham
The Old Brewery House Hotel

MAP: OS LANDRANGER 133 (GR 101229)	**WALK 14**	DISTANCE: 4 MILES

DIRECTIONS TO START: REEPHAM IS 7 MILES SOUTH-WEST OF AYLSHAM, ON THE B1145. THE PUB IS IN THE SQUARE IN THE CENTRE OF TOWN. **PARKING:** HEAD OUT OF THE MARKET PLACE WITH THE OLD BREWERY HOUSE ON YOUR LEFT, TAKE THE FIRST LEFT TURN AND FIRST LEFT AGAIN TO ENTER THE LARGE PUB CAR PARK.

Norfolk's unofficial motto 'do different' could have been coined for the attractive market town of Reepham. Its oval churchyard contains two medieval churches – St Mary's and St Michael's – touching each other, and the remains of a third, All Saints', destroyed by fire in 1543. The boundaries of three parishes meet here and it is assumed each wanted a church close to the developing market. The square ringed by handsome Georgian buildings is still a lively place on market day, and though the walk starts from the rear of the pub for convenience, the old town should not be missed. The focal point of this walk through open farmland is not, however, Reepham's churches but the magnificent church of SS Peter and Paul in the hamlet of Salle, claimed by many to be the finest in a county of fine churches.

There is also a short, attractive stretch along the old railway line before you re-enter the town.

The Old Brewery House Hotel

This large, comfortable and friendly pub-cum-hotel feels as if it has been in business for centuries, but it was only in 1972 that it was converted from a family home. Built in 1729 and originally named the Dial House – the sundial is still an impressive feature of the façade – it maintains a country house character with polished wooden floors and a variety of armchairs dotted about.

'Food is an important part of a balanced diet' – that is one of an array of quotations, old and new, funny and serious, chalked on a ceiling beam in the bar area. F. Leibowitz, the American columnist who wrote it, would have no fears about the balance at the Old Brewery House. A daily specials board has such dishes as seafood ragout with basmati rice and peppered beef with noodles, and the bar food list includes sausages and mash with Reepham Ale gravy – there is still a small brewery in the town. The evening menu is more adventurous, with such delights as duck breast on crispy sweet potato, and supreme of tuna with roasted Mediterranean vegetables. There is an excellent choice of vegetarian dishes.

Regular real ales are Adnams Best, Greene King Abbot and Reepham Bitter with guests from the local brewery. A key feature of the hotel is its leisure centre, with a pool, squash court, sauna and solarium. There are 23 ensuite rooms, four of them with four-poster beds. Telephone: 01603 870881.

The Walk

① Turn right out of the pub car park and left after 100 yards along a lane. Pass the Crown pub to meet a main road; cross, turn right and after 20 yards bear left up a path over the old railway. Keep straight ahead at a lane, with the tower of Salle (pronounced Saul) church soaring above trees ahead to the right.

② After 200 yards, where the lane bends left, enter the field on your right and turn left, following a fingerpost on a field-edge path close to the lane. After 300 yards turn right, with a fingerpost, passing to the right of a tall hedge. Just after a narrow conifer plantation, turn left on a path heading for the church.

③ After a further 300 yards turn right, following a yellow arrow alongside a hedge to meet a lane. Turn left and soon left again on a lane signed 'Salle Street' to the church. This massive and elegantly simple building is testimony to the wool trade wealth accrued by local families.

On the route

④ Opposite the church, pass to the right of a redbrick building with a Lynton White Institute plaque, turn left behind it and go diagonally right across the field to a large gap in the hedge. Turn right with a yellow arrow and soon you are retracing your steps ahead, right and left to the lane.

⑤ Head back towards Reepham and just after 30 mph signs turn right on World's End Lane, with a fingerpost. Follow a yellow arrow to the right of a hedge and then go over a stile. Keep on the path along the right-hand edge of the meadow, crossing a ditch to the far end. Turn left with a yellow arrow and soon climb a stile, cross the lane and climb steps to the old railway line – now the Marriott's Way path.

⑥ Turn left on the track and after 400 yards go up the platform of the old Reepham Station, now a tearoom. Pass behind it and follow the lane to the road; cross to the Crown and retrace your steps.

PLACES OF INTEREST NEARBY

Norfolk Wildlife Park at Great Witchingham on the A1067 south of Reepham is a family-orientated place with a good collection of European mammals and wildfowl in 40 acres of parkland. You can watch wild grey herons nesting and there is a model farm with tame animals and a commando adventure playground. It is open daily from 1 April to 31 October. Telephone: 01603 872274.

Weston Longville
The Parson Woodforde

MAP: OS LANDRANGER 133 (GR 114159)　　**WALK 15**　　**DISTANCE:** 3½ MILES

DIRECTIONS TO START: WESTON LONGVILLE IS ABOUT 6 MILES NORTH-WEST
OF NORWICH, JUST OFF THE A1067. THE PUB IS OPPOSITE THE CHURCH.
PARKING: IN THE PUB CAR PARK, WITH PERMISSION.

This village set in gently rolling countryside is noted as the setting for *The Diary of a Country Parson*, recording the tranquil yet fascinating life of its Rector, James Woodforde. It is a work still widely enjoyed as an insight into people's lives in the late 18th century – the farmers, servants, doctors, tradesmen and squires the Parson came in contact with. The second part of the village name came from Longeville priory in Normandy, to which its tithes were transferred at the turn of the 12th century by its Norman lord of the manor. Weston was a peaceful place in Woodforde's time, but not so during the Second World War when the airfield just outside the village was home to the 466th Bomber Group of the US Air Force. From March 1944 to May 1945, 324 men were killed while flying sorties from here, a statistic recorded on the village sign. The stroll takes in quiet lanes and footpaths the Parson himself, a keen walker, would doubtless have used.

The Parson Woodforde

The good Parson loved his food and loved writing about it. The *Diary* is full of lip-smacking references to huge meals of boiled and roasted meats, fish and game birds of all kinds. He would have approved of the food the pub offers today, though he never had the chance to enjoy its hospitality as it was built in 1824, some 20 years after his death. The village inn that was known to him, the White Hart, is now a private house.

The Parson Woodforde has the feel of a handsome country manor, with solid beams, exposed brick walls and large brick fireplaces. Food is freshly prepared using local game, meat and vegetables, and the bar menu features such dishes as sausage and mash, steak and kidney pie and fresh haddock or cod in Parson's Ale batter. A separate restaurant menu has a wider choice, including tournedos rossini topped with chicken liver pâté and madeira sauce; and roasted fillet of halibut with dill and cucumber butter sauce. Whisky and marmalade bread and butter pudding would surely have gone down well with the Parson.

Among regular real ales is the house bitter brewed by Woodforde's, an independent Norfolk firm set up in 1981 and named after the Parson, who used to brew his own ale. Woodforde's Wherry, Adnams Best and Broadside, Nethergate from Suffolk and a guest ale complete the line-up.

Families are welcome in a pleasant separate dining room and there is an attractive, hedged garden. Telephone: 01603 880106.

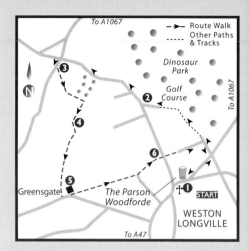

The Walk

① Turn left out of the pub and down the lane, signed 'Morton on the Hill' (something of a Norfolk joke, this – as in several similarly-named places, it is at most a gentle incline). After 200 yards turn left on Morton Lane, soon passing a golf course on the right.

② At the T-junction turn right. The road soon bends sharply left by a farm which has ostriches in paddocks, a fine example of farm diversification.

③ At the next crossroads turn left on Hockering Road and after 50 yards left on a public footpath – the fingerpost is across the road. The path is not clearly defined here, but walk diagonally uphill across the field, heading for the right-hand end of a line of trees. At the trees, turn left along the field edge and at the bottom of the slope turn right, keeping the hedge on your left.

④ After 200 yards turn left and climb a stile 50 yards ahead. Turn right up the hill with pleasant open country stretching away to your left, where horses enjoy the freedom

Farmland near Weston Longville

of extensive paddocks. After 150 yards climb a second stile. At the top of the field go through a wide gap in the hedge and keep straight ahead on a clear path through a field of crops, heading for a brick barn conversion. Circle the barn anti-clockwise and turn left in front of it.

⑤ Now keep straight ahead, following a yellow arrow sign. Cross a couple of fields and pass a pond ringed by trees over to the left. The path heads downhill with open country to the left.

⑥ Where the path meets a lane at right angles keep straight ahead (or to shorten the walk slightly, turn right here back into Weston Longville.) Pass a wood then a whitewashed, thatched cottage on the left.

Turn right at the junction with Morton Lane and retrace your route, turning right at the crossroads to return to the pub. Opposite, the plain-looking 14th century All Saints' church has a simple beauty inside, with a tile set into the floor marking Parson Woodforde's burial site.

PLACES OF INTEREST NEARBY
The Dinosaur Adventure Park signed off the A1067 just north of Weston Longville is a popular family attraction with realistic life-size models of dinosaurs set along woodland trails. There's also a Neanderthal village display, a well-equipped education centre, shop and café and good play equipment. It is open from around Easter to the end of October but times vary according to the month. Check by telephoning 01603 870245.

Wymondham
The Green Dragon

MAP: OS LANDRANGER 144 (GR 108016)   WALK 16   DISTANCE: 2¼ MILES

DIRECTIONS TO START: WYMONDHAM (PRONOUNCED WINDHAM) IS 9 MILES SOUTH-WEST OF NORWICH, JUST OFF THE A11. THE PUB IS ON CHURCH STREET, NEAR THE ABBEY. **PARKING:** IN THE PUB CAR PARK, WITH PERMISSION. THERE ARE SEVERAL FREE CAR PARKS NEARBY.

(Photo courtesy of S. Hill)

The great bulk of Wymondham Abbey with its twin towers and strange history looms over this gentle stroll by the River Tiffey. Founded in 1107 by William D'Albini, Chief Butler to King Henry I, it was intended to serve both a community of Benedictine monks and the townspeople. However, the rights of each were unclear and there were many quarrels, often concerning the hanging and ringing of parish bells. A practical, if extreme, solution was eventually found by the parishioners who erected their own great West Tower in 1445. The odd-shaped building (looking from a distance more like a power station than a church) dominates the skyline; this walk takes in its grounds and monastery ruins, but a look at its magnificent interior is recommended. The abbey was later dedicated to St Mary and St Thomas à Becket, and his influence is strong throughout this attractive medieval town.

The Green Dragon

This quaint 14th century inn can lay claim to be one of the dozen oldest in the country and possibly the oldest building in continuous retail use, having been a butcher's shop originally. It narrowly escaped destruction in the Great Fire of 1615 when many of the town's houses were destroyed and served as a hostelry for visitors to the abbey. It has a tiny, atmospheric interior with a beamed dining room and a wood-panelled snug with an open fireplace, a Tudor mantelpiece and a door in the corner bearing the faded words 'To the Abbey'. It is thought a 'monks' run' once led from a cellar under the bar to the abbey, for use by the supposedly teetotal monks.

The food is freshly made on the premises, and a range of traditional dishes includes Dragon Pie of braised British beef with mushrooms and Guinness, fillet steak with a creamy Stilton sauce and pan-fried tuna steak. There are always two or three vegetarian options. A daily lunchtime specials board might offer such dishes as chicken korma or mushroom and cashew nut stroganoff; there is also a children's menu. Food is served every day in summer, but not on Sunday evenings in winter.

Real ales are Adnams Broadside and Flowers IPA and you will also find Tetley bitter, draught Guinness, Stella and Scrumpy Jack cider. There is an attractive walled beer garden, and B&B accommodation in four double rooms plus a family room. Telephone: 01953 607907.

The Walk

① Turn left out of the pub and pass the library, dating from 1400 and on the site of the earlier Chapel of Thomas à Becket. A plaque marks Kett's Rebellion, a 1549 peasants' uprising against land enclosures led by Robert Kett, a local landowner sympathetic to their cause. He formed an army several thousand strong that marched on Norwich and was defeated only when the King sent a force from London. He was hanged from Norwich Castle and his brother, William, from the West Tower of Wymondham Abbey. Kett's Oak, a rallying point for the rebels, can still be seen just outside the town. Turn sharp right along Damgate Street, a medieval lane with several fine old houses.

② Immediately after crossing a bridge, turn right on a footpath by the River Tiffey. This opens out into a landscaped area and there is a splendid view of the abbey across meadowland.

③ Cross a lane (this point is known as Becket's Well though the well itself is on private land) and through a small car park

The bulk of Wymondham Abbey dominates the walk

opposite. Go through a wooden gate and along a footpath by the river. On the left is Abbey Halt station – the railway line to Dereham has only recently been reopened. The Tiffey now flows clear and bright across meadowland with butterbur and lesser celandine clothing its banks in season.

④ After ½ mile, and just before the path crosses the rail line, turn right across a wooden footbridge over the river, following a red 'circular walks' arrow. Turn right and head diagonally across a damp meadow towards the hedge line. With a ditch on your left, keep straight ahead with the abbey now prominent again. Climb a stile and the path becomes a track leading to a road.

⑤ Turn right on Chapel Lane and head back into town, passing several more half-timbered houses. Turn right on Vicar Street just before the war memorial. For a tour of

the abbey, turn right on Becketswell Road for 100 yards and then left through a gate, or turn left on Church Street to return to the pub.

PLACES OF INTEREST NEARBY

Wymondham Heritage Museum at the Bridewell in the centre of town is in the former jail built in 1783 after recommendations by prison reformer John Howard. The old cells are still in place, and there is a display on penal reform. There is also an interesting exhibition on brush-making, a key industry in the town. The museum, with a café, is open from 1 March to 30 November, Monday to Saturday 10 am to 4 pm and Sunday 2 pm to 4 pm. Telephone: 01953 600205.

Wymondham Station on the edge of town has carefully-restored buildings and displays of railway memorabilia. Its Brief Encounter restaurant is designed like a train carriage with many posters and old timetables on the walls.

New Buckenham
The King's Head

MAP: OS LANDRANGER 144 (GR 087904) **WALK 17** **DISTANCE:** 2½ MILES

DIRECTIONS TO START: NEW BUCKENHAM IS 16 MILES SOUTH-WEST OF NORWICH, ON THE B1113. THE KING'S HEAD IS IN THE CENTRE OF THE VILLAGE OVERLOOKING THE GREEN. **PARKING:** THE PUB HAS NO CAR PARK BUT THERE IS FREE PARKING AROUND THE VILLAGE GREEN.

Modern only when compared with nearby Old Buckenham, and still more than 800 years old, New Buckenham is unique in England as a medieval planned town. William D'Albini chose the site for his new castle in 1145, and the village was laid out on a grid of intersecting streets to the east. This pattern remains unchanged and the tightly-knit streets are lined with 15th to 17th century timber-frame houses, some faced in brick, some in different colour washes.

This walk takes in the village with its 'uncommonly sumptuous' church – Pevsner's words – of St Martin, a light and airy structure which like so many in Norfolk seems too magnificent for the size of the village, testimony to the county's former wealth. You then circle the ruined castle in its tranquil, leafy setting and head out over the extensive Common which is still lightly grazed by cattle kept by owners of grazing rights.

The King's Head

When Cromwell was in power he closed two of the village inns because the ale they brewed was too strong – it wasn't so much the alcohol content that upset him but that they were using too much grain that could have gone to bread-making.

New Buckenham is lucky, compared with other villages of its size, still to have two pubs in operation. The King's Head is much the older, dating from before 1645 when it was a coaching inn on the Norwich road and later well used by cattle drovers. It has a small, traditional interior of two beamed rooms, one with a stone-flagged floor, and a homely atmosphere.

The food is traditional, home-cooked pub fare such as beef with mustard sauce, and steak, onion and mushroom ale pie, with several more unusual dishes including Oriental pork with rice, and salmon in gooseberry sauce. There is also a good choice of vegetarian dishes – Cajun vegetable casserole, three-cheese and broccoli pasta bake and chilli non carne among them. There is no food on Mondays.

The pub is a freehouse with draught Bass and Adnams Best Bitter as its 'house beers' plus regular real ales from the independent Iceni brewery in Norfolk, whose Red, White and Blueberry Ale was on offer when I called.

Children are welcome in the pub, and outside in summer there are tables in a small paved courtyard. B&B accommodation is available. Telephone: 01953 860487.

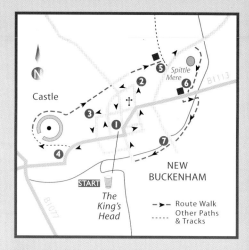

The Walk

① Walk straight ahead from the pub down a lane to the right of the Market House. This was a court or toll house whose whipping post, complete with arm clamps, is still in place. Turn left at the end of the lane and keep straight ahead across the road, passing the early 19th century village forge with the words 'Holls Veterinary Shoeing Forge' just visible.

② Turn left and left again to circle the church, passing both the George and the King's Head. Turn right on King Street past Tudor Rose Cottage with its 1738 plaque and initials IEL (Joseph and Elizabeth Lucas). Turn right on Rosemary Lane and then left into Chapel Street.

③ Turn left back to King Street and then right, passing Castle Hill Garage. If you wish to visit the castle grounds themselves – well worth it for the path round its impressive earthworks and remains of the earliest circular keep in the country – you must get the key from the garage (the charge is currently £1) and return it before continuing on your walk.

New Buckenham's ruined castle

④ To continue the walk, just past the garage take the footpath to the right, which follows the castle moat clockwise. Cross a road and head past the village hall on your left.

⑤ After the playing field turn right on a concrete track and then left for 100 yards on a lane before going through a metal gate on your right and onto a grassy path across the Common. Pass to the left of Spittle Mere and then turn right on a slightly raised path towards a pink-washed house.

⑥ Go through a wooden gate to the main road and turn left. After 75 yards climb a stile on the right then turn immediately right and left when you reach a stream. Keep close to the stream, across a plank bridge, heading towards a larger wooden bridge with handrail. Don't cross the bridge but go straight ahead over two stiles and then right along the field edge.

⑦ Turn left at a track and immediately right over a stile with a yellow arrow sign. Keep ahead on the field edge, over a stile and turn right up a grassy track which becomes Marsh Lane, back into the village.

PLACES OF INTEREST NEARBY

Banham Zoo by the B1113 south-west of New Buckenham is well laid out in 30 acres of landscaped gardens, with a good collection of rare animals, and takes part in international breeding programmes for such species as snow leopard. There is a Heritage Farm Centre with shire horses and horse dray rides, and a Tarzan Trail play area with good equipment. There is also a shop, café and Banham Cidery where you can watch cider pressing. The zoo is open daily from 10 am except Christmas Day and Boxing Day. Telephone: 01953 887771.

Upper Sheringham
The Red Lion

MAP: OS LANDRANGER 133 (GR 146419)   **WALK 18**   **DISTANCE:** 2¼ MILES

DIRECTIONS TO START: UPPER SHERINGHAM IS JUST OUTSIDE SHERINGHAM, OFF THE A148. COMING FROM HOLT, TAKE THE SIGNED MINOR ROAD LEFT AFTER BODHAM. THE PUB IS IN THE CENTRE OF THE VILLAGE **PARKING:** IN THE CAR PARK OPPOSITE THE PUB, WITH PERMISSION.

lint cottages with red pantiled roofs, neat flint-walled gardens crammed with flowers – Upper Sheringham will be many people's idea of a typical Norfolk village. Set in the coastal Area of Outstanding Natural Beauty also known rather more poetically as Poppyland, it was the main settlement when the nearby resort of Sheringham was a mere fishing village. The walk takes in the delightful National Trust-owned (but with no charge for visitors on foot) Sheringham Park, with its wooded slopes and not over-manicured grassland. Best known for spectacular displays of rhododendrons and azaleas in late May and early June, it has much more to offer than that, including marked walks ranging from 1 mile to 5¼ miles and well-placed viewing points in this, the highest area of Norfolk. The park – and thus the walk – is open from sunrise to sunset round the year.

The Red Lion

Traditional simplicity is the keynote at this 400-year-old freehouse. A plain flint exterior leads to two welcoming rooms – the main bar with original 'pamment' tiles and the wooden-floored snug. The Red Lion claims the deepest pub cellar in Norfolk, with a blacksmith said to haunt it, and is keen to point out that there are no fruit machines, juke box, piped music or pool tables to upset the old boy.

On the food front, too, there is a declaration of intent. No standard menu but an ever-changing blackboard, no chips, no sandwiches – just freshly made dishes using local ingredients. Seafood is naturally a speciality, with its own board: Sheringham crab or lobster, Morston mussels, halibut and trout, plus more exotic shark and swordfish steaks, with Stiffkey samphire in season. Game comes 'from woods and fields surrounding the pub', most of the meat from a neighbouring farm and puffballs are gathered locally.

Popular dishes are steak and Norfolk ale pie and – keeping up with food fashions – Thai-style red chicken curry. There are always at least three veggie options. No Sunday evening food in winter and – more simplicity – no credit cards.

Regular beers are Woodforde's Wherry and Greene King IPA, plus a summer guest. The Red Lion boasts one of the largest whisky collections of any pub – more than 60 single malts.

There is a particularly attractive walled garden and overnight accommodation in one double and two twin rooms. Telephone: 01263 825408.

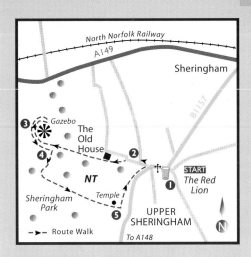

The Walk

① Turn left out of the pub and pass All Saints' church with, in front of it, the spring-fed pond that locals call the 'Reservoir'. Built in 1814 by Squire Abbot Upcher to mark peace in the Napoleonic Wars – a celebration premature by a year as it turned out – it was Upper Sheringham's main domestic water supply until the mid-1950s. Where the main road bends sharply left, keep ahead on Park Road and at the next junction continue into Sheringham Park.

② Go through the metal gate and along the main drive. To the right there are views to the sea and Beeston Bump, which lays claim to being Norfolk's highest point. Shortly after Sheringham Hall, still a private house not open to the public, keep straight ahead on a grassy track that leaves the metalled roadway, following a sign to the Gazebo viewing point.

③ Go through a wooden gate and turn right along the field edge. After 200 yards turn right, following the Gazebo sign, up a wooded hillside with steps. This is probably

Upcher's Temple

④ Continue up the hill on the surfaced roadway through attractive grassland. The path bends left with large areas of rhododendrons and azaleas on the right. At the first crossroads of paths turn left past a stump marked with red, blue and orange arrows and walk downhill in a pine and bracken-clad valley.

⑤ Go through a wooden gate and uphill to the white stone Thomas Upcher's Temple viewpoint. Pass to the right of the temple and keep straight ahead on a grassy track which bends left and continues downhill to the park gate. Retrace your steps to the pub.

PLACES OF INTEREST NEARBY

Norfolk Shire Horse Centre, at West Runton between Sheringham and Cromer, has heavy horses working daily, mares with foals, a children's farm and free cart rides for children. It is open from around the beginning of April to the end of October, but closed most Saturdays. Times vary, check by telephoning 01263 837339.

North Norfolk Railway is a full-scale steam and diesel railway along the coast between Sheringham, Weybourne and Holt. Day return tickets allow you to break your journey and explore – for details telephone Sheringham Station, which links with mainline services, on 01263 822045.

the stiffest climb in the whole book but well worth it for the chance to ascend the Gazebo – a misleading name for it is in fact a tower taking you up above the treetops with magnificent views to the coast. Away to the left is the village of Weybourne and beyond that, on a clear day, Blakeney Point 9 miles away.

Now retrace your steps, back through the wooden gate to the first Gazebo sign and turn right.

Wolterton

The Saracen's Head

MAP: OS LANDRANGER 133 (GR 171323)   **WALK 19**   **DISTANCE:** 2 MILES

DIRECTIONS TO START: THE PUB STANDS ON A MINOR ROAD 4 MILES NORTH-WEST OF AYLSHAM. THE NEAREST VILLAGE IS CALTHORPE, ½ MILE TO THE EAST. WOLTERTON IS NOT ON MOST ROAD ATLASES, CONSISTING ALMOST ENTIRELY OF THE HALL AND PARK. FROM THE A140 TURN OFF WESTWARDS 4 MILES NORTH OF AYLSHAM FOLLOWING A 'WOLTERTON PARK' SIGN THROUGH ERPINGHAM AND CALTHORPE. **PARKING:** IN THE PUB CAR PARK, WITH PERMISSION.

'Lost in North Norfolk' is how the Saracen's Head positions itself and there is, indeed, a feeling of remoteness on this walk's quiet lanes and paths, which pass only an occasional redbrick cottage along the way. Wolterton Hall – built in the 1720s by Thomas Ripley for Horatio Walpole, younger brother of the great statesman Sir Robert – and its Park are nearby but they are hidden from view and they do not, in any case, attract hordes of visitors.

This is no chilling kind of remoteness that you will find, however, nothing bleak or even slightly sinister. It's more like stepping back in time to a patch of rural Norfolk that has largely escaped modern development, a secluded corner where the sun seems to shine more often than elsewhere and the hedgerows, fruit and flower-filled in season, are left more to their own devices.

The Saracen's Head

There is a noble origin to this distinctive country inn, built in 1806 as a coach house for the Walpoles and modelled on a Tuscan farmhouse. It was long known as Wolterton New Inn – Wolterton Hall is just across the road – and the present name was adopted around the 1930s since a saracen's head features on the crest of the Walpoles, who had fought in the Crusades.

There is certainly a casually Italian flavour, in the delightful courtyard and tall-windowed rooms warmed by the reds and terracottas of the décor. The pub enjoys being off-track and off-beat – no piped music or fruit machines, no chips, peas or scampi, it declares. The constantly changing blackboard menu has a quirky style too, but there is nothing haphazard about the food, as a string of awards testify.

Using mainly local ingredients, the dishes have a twist setting them apart from standard pub fare – pan-fried liver of venison with red fruit; escalope of lamb in oatmeal and cranberry jus; baked crab with mushroom, sherry and cream. Starters can be taken as main course portions, good news for vegetarians with offerings such as grilled goat's cheese with Mediterranean vegetables and crispy fried aubergine with garlic mayonnaise.

There are always two real ales, one from Woodforde's, though there is more wine than beer by volume sold here, with 24 bottles on the list. Booking is advisable at any time, and there are four guest rooms for overnight accommodation. Telephone: 01263 768909.

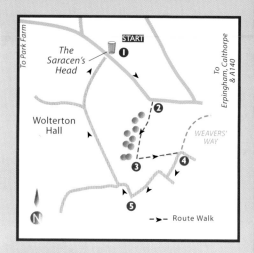

The Walk

① Turn left out of the pub and along the lane, with open farmland on both sides. As you look back at the Saracen's Head, you can now appreciate its unusual position, surrounded by fields.

② After about 500 yards, where the lane bends left, turn right following a public footpath sign towards a wood. The path skirts round to the left of the trees and heads down a broad, grassy strip keeping close to the wood, with good views of typical rolling North Norfolk countryside.

③ At the end of the wood, turn 90 degrees left on an unsigned path along a field edge between two fields of crops, heading in the direction of a distant church tower. After 200 yards, at the end of the field, turn right by a couple of ancient farm wagons and immediately left on a track.

④ Turn right when this meets a lane, where there is a yellow County Council arrow pointing back the way you have come (so why isn't there one at the turn by the wood?). Follow this quiet lane, part of the

Harvest time near the Saracen's Head pub

Weavers' Way, as it leads between two cottages and bends sharply right then left. Blackberries, wild plums and a variety of flowers enrich the hedgerows along this stretch in season and butterflies will often keep you company as you walk.

⑤ The lane bends right and left again, passing a brick cottage on the right. After 50 yards turn right on a track with a public bridleway marker and, most conveniently, a sign directing you towards the Saracen's Head. This pleasant track leads gradually uphill between mature oaks at first, then with open arable countryside on your right before passing an isolated house with a lovely cottage garden. After the track bends slightly right, the pub makes a welcome appearance, framed by trees, in the distance straight ahead. The path leads between trees to spill you out directly opposite the front door.

PLACES OF INTEREST NEARBY

Alby Crafts on the A140 between Aylsham and Cromer is an interesting collection of craft workshops based in traditional brick and flint farm buildings. Painting, glassmaking, pottery and knitwear are among the skills that can be seen, and there is also a lace museum and an excellent bottle museum. The attractive grounds include a bee garden with hives. From mid-March to mid-December it is open Tuesdays to Sundays 10 am to 5 pm; from mid-January to mid-March, weekends only. Telephone: 01263 761590.

Wolterton Hall and Park are owned by Lord and Lady Walpole. The gardens are open daily from 9 am to dusk and the hall offers tours every Friday from around the end of April, last tour 4 pm. Telephone 01263 584175 for exact dates and times.

Blickling
The Buckinghamshire Arms

MAP: OS LANDRANGER 133 (GR 177286)   **WALK 20**   **DISTANCE:** 2¼ MILES

DIRECTIONS TO START: BLICKLING IS ON THE B1354 A MILE NORTH-WEST OF
AYLSHAM. THE PUB IS ON A LANE A FEW YARDS FROM THE MAIN ROAD, TURN RIGHT
JUST PAST BLICKLING HALL. **PARKING:** IN THE PUB CAR PARK, WITH PERMISSION.

Norfolk can boast some of the most splendid country estates in Britain, and Blickling – now owned by the National Trust – is right up there with the best. The elegant Hall was built for Sir Henry Hobart, Lord Chief Justice, in 1619-27 on the site of an earlier house where Anne Boleyn spent her early years. Her ghost, carrying head on lap of course, is said to be driven up to the Hall in a coach every May 19, the anniversary of her execution. The parkland surrounding the Hall is no less magnificent and offers a variety of strolls among wooded slopes, open farmland and by a lovely crescent-shaped lake. There is also that touch of English eccentricity in the forbidding, grey-stone pyramid mausoleum of the 2nd Earl of Buckinghamshire, a title bestowed on the Hobart family by this time. He was ambassador to Russia, and in the Hall is a tapestry of Peter the Great at the battle of Poltowa, given him by Catherine the Great.

The Buckinghamshire Arms

This handsome Jacobean inn came into being as part of the Blickling estate and still owes much of its business to the stream of visitors to the magnificent Hall. Built in 1693 for estate bricklayer John Balls – and he doubtless helped construct it – the 'Bucks' was later used to house the servants of the growing number of noble guests. It was substantially rebuilt in its present form in the mid-18th century, when it also became an inn.

Inside there's a strong period feel, the quaint front snug looking more or less unaltered. There's a comfortable lounge area with open fireplace, a slightly more formal dining room and a farmhouse kitchen-style parlour that welcomes families with children. The fact that many of the customers have the visit to Blickling in common creates a convivial atmosphere which the friendly staff encourage.

Working entirely from a blackboard, the food is freshly cooked using local ingredients and has a homely flavour – most popular dishes are homemade sausage and herb pie, and steak and kidney pie; veggie options include potato and leek crumble. The lunchtime menu tends to be lighter, with dishes such as smoked salmon and prawn pasta, and chicken breast in tarragon sauce.

Real ales include Blickling brewed by Woodforde's especially for the pub and Greene King IPA and Abbot. Outside there is a lovely beer garden served by a hatch from the snug.

Overnight accommodation is available, fittingly, in three period rooms with four-poster beds and views of Blickling Hall. Telephone: 01263 732133.

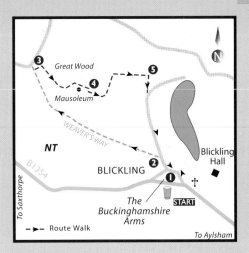

The Walk

① Turn left out of the pub, following a red arrow along the lane past several attractive cottages and gardens. The lane bends right and leads through gates into Blickling Park. Here there is a map of the estate with a variety of marked trails, the longer ones taking in the lake with views to the rear of the Hall.

② Turn almost immediately left, following the red arrow up a broad track through parkland dotted with mature oak and sweet chestnut trees. Go through a wooden gate and at the top of the slope keep straight ahead, ignoring a red arrowed path to the right. Now on the left a tall, brick tower comes into view – apparently once used as a vantage point to watch horse races held here. The track now leads downhill through trees.

③ Just before a wooden gate turn right, across a short stretch of grass, to a footpath backed by trees. Now turn right, ignoring a broader path to the left and head up into Great Wood. Keep climbing, ignoring a minor path off to the right, and you will

65

The 17th century Blickling Hall

soon reach a clearing where the ground levels out. Take a fairly narrow path heading diagonally left to a large pyramid-shaped mausoleum that can be clearly seen through the trees. A plaque gives the history of this strange construction, which seems at odds with its woodland setting.

④ Pass the pyramid and head down a broad, grassy ride. At a junction of paths take the second left, which has red and blue arrow markers. Turn right at the next path junction then straight ahead over a stile with open farmland now on the left.

⑤ The path bends left through trees then after 50 yards right, with the red arrow. (For a longer walk down to the lake you can follow the blue arrow at this point.) Go

through a wooden gate with a stile option and head straight ahead on the track with fine views down to the lake on your left. At the park gates retrace your steps to the pub.

PLACES OF INTEREST NEARBY

Blickling Hall is one of the finest Jacobean houses in the country, its best-known feature being the remarkable Long Gallery which was built for 'social activity and indoor exercise' and was used as a library from 1745 onwards. A range of opulent rooms hold fine furniture, paintings and tapestries. The house and gardens are open from the beginning of April to the end of October, Wednesdays to Sundays and the gardens also from November to mid-December. Telephone 01263 734181 for exact times. The park and woods are always open from dawn to dusk.

Mulbarton
The World's End

DIRECTIONS TO START: MULBARTON IS 6 MILES SOUTH-WEST OF NORWICH ON THE B1113. APPROACHING FROM THE NORTH, THE PUB IS ON THE RIGHT OF THE MAIN ROAD ON THE EDGE OF THE VILLAGE. **PARKING:** IN THE LARGE PUB CAR PARK.

It is unusual in such a heavily cultivated county as Norfolk to find much in the way of 'wild' landscape, except on the coastal strip. This walk, however, manages largely to achieve this goal as it meanders along the undeveloped valley of the River Tas, with its rough grazing and light woodland, only a few miles south of Norwich. It also takes in the attractive village of Swardeston, birthplace of the nurse Edith Cavell, who became a national heroine during the First World War when she was shot by a German firing squad for sheltering Allied soldiers and helping them escape from Belgium. The British public was outraged and huge crowds attended her memorial service at Westminster Abbey – such a contrast from the quiet village where she grew up and the tranquil churchyard where her father, the Vicar of Swardeston, and mother are buried.

The World's End

In the 1700s, if one was walking out from Norwich, the village of Mulbarton no doubt did seem like the end of the world as there were few settlements for some distance ahead. That, anyway, is how locals believe the pub got its name – one of some eight in the country to be so called. There was a coaching inn on the site about 300 years ago – this was the last stop before Norwich – though the present building is probably around 130 years old.

It has a resident ghost, Lavinia, a serving girl who worked at the inn and was murdered by a traveller whose advances she resisted. She is held responsible for occasional banging noises, ashtrays thrown to the floor and pictures falling from walls.

The World's End nowadays is comfortable, traditionally-styled and family-orientated, offering good-value home-cooked pub grub with favourites like gammon steak, battered cod and sirloin steak. A specials board changing daily has a wider range with dishes such as surf and turf, minted lamb fillet and mushroom and pepper stroganoff. There is always a vegetarian special. Food is served seven days a week and there is a separate restaurant. The pub is open all day on Saturdays and Sundays.

Tied to the Adnams brewery, the pub has its award-winning Best Bitter and also Boddingtons, Caffreys, Carlsberg, Carling, Stella and draught Guinness.

There is an unusually large and pleasant beer garden with an excellent play area, and for overnight accommodation there are two ensuite guest rooms. Telephone: 01508 570205.

The Walk

① Turn left out of the pub along the main road and go left down Catbridge Lane. After 300 yards turn right through a gate in a wooden fence, following a Tas Valley Way sign. The path goes through a pleasant area of young trees and damp meadow where green woodpeckers can often be heard.

② The path bends right then left to cross a wooden footbridge by ponds. Follow the path round to the left, through a small wood and into a field. Go through a wide hedge gap and straight along the field bottom, ignoring one path to the left and then, 100 yards further on, turn left through a wooden kissing gate and follow the Tas Valley sign to the right.

③ Walk along an area of rough grazing, through another kissing gate and at the end of a field turn right, through a third wooden gate. Turn left on a track and after 50 yards cross a lane following a fingerpost. The path leads through a 'tunnel' of woodland and opens out into a green lane. Where this meets a road by a house, turn right on The Common.

The tranquil River Tas

④ Walk up the lane passing Cavell House, Edith's birthplace. At a junction cross the road and turn right up the unsurfaced High Common. Pass Swardeston cricket ground, turn right at the lane and almost immediately left on a gravel track signed 'The Vicarage', into the churchyard.

⑤ The delightful church of St Mary the Virgin (open daily, 10 am to 5 pm) has photographs and other memorabilia of Edith Cavell. Go through a lychgate at the top of the churchyard, turn right by the war memorial bearing her name and pass between white posts, following a green arrow signed 'Kett's Country' (see Walk 16). The path bends right past a beautiful Georgian house with a moated garden.

⑥ Turn left, go through a barred gate and keep straight ahead following Kett's Country signs for ¾ mile until the path rejoins Catbridge Lane. Turn left and then right on the main road to return to the pub.

PLACES OF INTEREST NEARBY

Caistor St Edmund, just off the A140 north-east of Mulbarton, has the site of the Roman settlement of Venta Icenorum, which 1,700 years ago was a major local government centre, a prosperous market town and the capital of Norfolk. It is one of the few Roman town sites in Britain not damaged or hidden by later buildings and has a town wall still standing to a height of 20 ft. There is a circular walk including such oddities as the footprint of a Roman labourer pressed into the mortar on top of a wall. The English Heritage site is open all the time.

Pulham Market
The Crown Inn

MAP: OS LANDRANGER 156 (GR 197862) · **WALK 22** · **DISTANCE:** 3¾ MILES

DIRECTIONS TO START: PULHAM MARKET IS ON THE B1134, 12 MILES SOUTH OF NORWICH AND 1 MILE EAST OF THE A140. THE PUB IS IN THE VILLAGE CENTRE, NEXT TO THE GREEN. **PARKING:** IN THE PUB CAR PARK.

Starting from the attractive, thatched-roof village of Pulham Market, this walk takes in proof that pigs did indeed once fly. These were the 'Pulham Pigs' – small airships so called because of their pinkish-buff envelopes – which flew from a base at neighbouring Pulham St Mary in the First World War to spot German submarines in the North Sea. The name stuck even when the colour was changed to silver for the larger commercial airships such as the R34 pictured on the village sign, which made the first double crossing of the Atlantic in 1919 and returned to Pulham in triumph. Pulham Market's village sign is also an interesting one, with its four shields representing the village's pubs – two of which, the Crown and the Falcon, still remain. The Queen's Head and the oddly-named Duck's Foot are, sadly, no more. The walk also includes a short stretch of the newly opened Boudica's Way, then on quiet lanes and through meadowland with a *Watership Down*-style population of rabbits.

The Crown Inn

This picture-postcard-pretty pub, in a lovely position overlooking the village green, dates back to the early 17th century. Not far from the Suffolk border, where thatch becomes much more common, it has a fine roof complete with straw cats and pheasant to complement the low, whitewashed walls.

Inside it is just as attractive, its one long room heavily beamed and divided by half-walls into smaller areas with comfortable furniture and cosy corners decorated with a wealth of interesting old pictures and photographs. Large brick fireplaces offer a welcome blaze in winter. At the back is a long extension that doubles as a function room and Sunday carvery restaurant.

Food here veers towards the traditional, home-made using fresh vegetables and local suppliers. Pies are a speciality, including steak and ale, turkey and leek, shepherd's pie and steak and kidney suet pudding. Cod in beer batter is also a favourite. There is always a good vegetarian choice, with dishes such as pancakes filled with wild mushrooms; roasted vegetables layered in tomato sauce; and three-cheese mornay. The Crown has a reputation as a good beer pub, with Adnams Best Bitter served from the firkin, one of few pubs still to do it this way. There are always two or three guest ales, including favourites such as Woodforde's Wherry, Timothy Taylor's Landlord and Fuller's London Pride.

There is an attractive beer garden overlooking the green. Telephone: 01379 676652.

The Walk

① Cross the green and pass to the right of the Falcon, through a white-painted fence with the Old Bakery on your right. Head down Church Walk to the lane, cross and take a track with a Boudica's Way marker. After 100 yards the path narrows between hedges to the left of a bungalow and continues on a footbridge over a ditch.

② Walk along the field edge and after 50 yards turn sharp right, ignoring the Boudica's Way sign straight ahead and keeping the hedge on your right. At the field corner, fork right into a copse and bear left following a yellow arrow. The path bends right across a footbridge then left on a plank bridge and through a narrow field of crops.

③ Turn left on a pleasant and little-used lane, which bends right to a junction, where you turn right on Poppy's Lane, signed 'Pulham St Mary'.

④ At the main road, turn left and then shortly right on Station Road by the village sign and King's Head. Walk through a

Thatched cottages around the village green

small modern estate and bear left, still on Station Road, at the junction.

⑤ A few yards after Willow Barn, turn right on an unsigned grassy track between hedges. Go over a stile and through a metal gate, bearing slightly right and then left on a shady path between tall hedges. After 100 yards turn right through a hedge gap and left along the meadow, keeping close to the stream on your right.

After about 200 yards go through a hedge gap and turn diagonally left away from the stream to meet the bed of the old railway line. Turn right on this. After a few yards go over a stile, turning right following a yellow arrow and then left just before a concrete bridge along a field-edge path. Cross a metal bridge with yellow arrow posts, then turn right and left alongside the stream.

⑥ Cross a footbridge over the stream, go ahead and then bear left with the arrows to the lane. Turn right and then go through the churchyard of St Mary Magdalene to emerge alongside the pub.

PLACES OF INTEREST NEARBY

Norfolk and Suffolk Aviation Museum at Flixton, just off the B1062 south-west of Bungay, has an impressive display of historic aircraft and also houses the museums of RAF Bomber Command, the Royal Observer Corps and the 446th Bomb Group as a tribute to the key role played by East Anglian airbases during the Second World War. Admission is free and the museum is open from April to October, Sunday to Thursday 10 am to 5 pm (last admission 4 pm) and from November to March, Tuesdays, Wednesdays and Sundays 10 am to 4 pm. Telephone: 01986 896644 or 01986 892696.

Buxton
The Buxton Mill Hotel

| **MAP:** OS LANDRANGER 134 (GR 238228) | **WALK 23** | **DISTANCE:** 2½ MILES |

DIRECTIONS TO START: BUXTON IS 9 MILES NORTH OF NORWICH, ON THE B1354. THE PUB IS ON A MINOR ROAD LEADING EASTWARDS OUT OF THE VILLAGE TOWARDS LAMAS, ON THE LEFT JUST AFTER CROSSING THE RIVER. **PARKING:** IN THE LARGE CAR PARK OPPOSITE THE MILL.

In sharp contrast to many stretches of river in Norfolk that are busy with boat traffic, the Bure in its upper reaches beyond Coltishall is a tranquil, meandering watercourse with cattle grazing beside it much as they have done for centuries. This walk starts at a picturesque 18th century mill between Buxton and Lamas (where *Black Beauty* author Anna Sewell lies in the Quaker Burial Ground) and goes on to capture the essence of timelessness in the Bure Valley, where the peace is only occasionally shattered, rather incongruously, by jets taking off from the nearby RAF airbase.

Because of lush vegetation by the river, especially in late spring and early summer, this is a walk best not done after heavy rain – or wearing shorts. There are also other excellent riverside walks north of Buxton Mill and along the footpath beside the Bure Valley Railway.

The Buxton Mill Hotel

This imposing former corn mill was built in 1754, though there had been a mill on the site since the 11th century when it had a Domesday mention as part of Buxton Manor, given to Ralph de Beaufour by William the Conqueror. There is a timeless quality about the tall building in its delightful setting by the Bure, but less than 10 years ago it was virtually destroyed by fire and what you see now is a careful restoration. In the process a stylish 14-bed hotel was created with an attractive beamed and tile-floored bar/restaurant and conservatory overlooking the mill stream.

The emphasis, in the restaurant and on the daily bar specials board, is on fresh Norfolk produce, with locally caught fish, game from neighbouring estates and herbs from a nearby garden. Dishes include duckling in sweet plum sauce, grilled Lowestoft plaice with rondelles of crab butter, and pan-fried scallops of pork fillet in pear brandy. There is also a good range of vegetarian dishes on offer, including crispy vegetable stir fry, three-bean chilli and vegetable parcel with a mild Thai curry sauce.

There is a local slant to the real ales, too. Wherry bitter and Norkie strong ale from Woodforde's are regulars, while Timberwolf and Granny Wouldn't Like It are the usual offerings from the independent Wolf brewery at Attleborough. Occasional guests include Adnams Best and Spitfire.

The pub is open all day and there is a small beer garden in a peaceful position overlooking the mill pond. Telephone: 01603 278194.

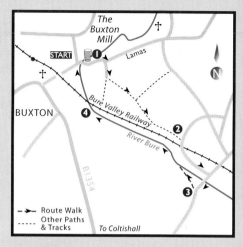

The Walk

① Turn left out of the pub and follow the lane by the river. After about 200 yards turn right on a dead-end lane following a public footpath sign. This leads gradually uphill and then bends left to become a broad track following a yellow arrow. There is now a pleasant view across crop fields and water meadows to the River Bure, and you may catch a glimpse of a train on the narrow-gauge Bure Valley Railway, a popular tourist track which runs for 9 miles from Aylsham to Wroxham. Ignore all paths to left and right as the track now leads downhill and bends to the right.

② Where the path meets a concrete track, turn right and go through metal gates across the railway line into a farmyard. Now turn left along a gravel track with an attractive Elizabethan manor house on your right. At the road turn right and cross a bridge over the gently flowing river. A warning to those of a nervous disposition – the airbase of RAF Coltishall is now very close to your left, hidden beyond a slope, and fighter jets take off from time to time, noisily but spectacularly, before twisting

The River Bure

away out of sight. That slope below the airfield is a favourite hunting ground for swifts, whose aerial manoeuvres as they dash and swoop for insects easily outperform the planes, to my mind.

③ Immediately after the bridge turn right following a public footpath sign through buttercup meadows along the river bank. The path is not very clearly defined here, but keep close to the river, through a field and over two wooden bridges. Vegetation, including nettles, can be dense at certain times of the year as the path follows a tranquil stretch of the river where swans glide and an occasional heron lifts itself, pterodactyl-like, from the reeds and flaps slowly away.

④ As the going becomes easier, turn right on a wooden bridge to pass under the rail line, then left across another bridge and along a good path by the river, back to the Mill.

PLACES OF INTEREST NEARBY

Wroxham Barns, signed off the A1151 at Wroxham, south-east of Buxton, is a collection of 14 craft workshops, including glassmaking, boatbuilding, pottery and basketry. There is also a traditional funfair with rides and a junior farm with chicks, guinea pigs and rabbits where children can collect eggs and groom ponies. Open all the year round from 10 am to 5 pm except Christmas Day and Boxing Day. Telephone: 01603 783762.

The Bure Valley Railway is a 9-mile narrow-gauge steam railway running between Aylsham and Wroxham and calling at Buxton. There are steam loco driving courses and also combined rail trips and Broads cruises. It is open from Easter to the end of October. Telephone: 01263 733858.

Norwich
The Adam and Eve

MAP: OS LANDRANGER 134 (GR 236092) OR A STREET MAP OF NORWICH

WALK 24

DISTANCE: 2½ MILES

DIRECTIONS TO START: THE PUB IS JUST OFF BISHOPGATE TO THE NORTH-WEST OF NORWICH CITY CENTRE. FROM THE INNER RING ROAD, FOLLOW SIGNS TO THE CATHEDRAL AT THE ROUNDABOUT NEAR ANGLIA SQUARE AND TURN LEFT ON BISHOPGATE JUST AFTER THE COURTS. **PARKING:** THERE IS A PAY-AND-DISPLAY CAR PARK AT ST HELEN'S WHARF OPPOSITE THE PUB.

A fine city – that was the assessment of Norwich by Victorian author George Borrow, of *Lavengro* fame and a regular customer at the Adam and Eve. It's a slogan still used to welcome visitors to the city and one which this walk will show is well merited. It takes in a leafy stretch of the River Wensum and heads past medieval buildings to the magnificent cathedral, which has the second highest spire in the country after Salisbury. A detour here is a must. From there it heads past the handsome bulk of the Norman castle to the colourful market, where the splendid, airy St Peter Mancroft church, the 'love it or loathe it' 1920s City Hall and the chequered flint-faced Guildhall are ranged behind. Shopping streets, quiet lanes and another stretch of the Riverside Walk take you back to the pub.

The Adam and Eve

This lovely pub, the oldest in Norwich, was mentioned as early as 1249 when it was a brewhouse for the workmen building Norwich Cathedral. Built round a Saxon well, which is still there beneath the lower bar floor, its living accommodation and Flemish gables were added in the 14th and 15th centuries. It has a colourful history and can claim several ghosts, including that of Lord Sheffield, hacked to death by peasants in Kett's Rebellion (see Walk 16). Among its many characters over the years was a mid-19th century landlady called Mrs Howes, who smuggled contraband in loads of sand for the pub floor which were brought from Yarmouth in her wherry, also named the Adam and Eve.

The pub today is full of atmosphere in its beamed and low-ceilinged rooms and, as befits such an ancient inn, offers an enticing range of food and drink. Among the dishes on offer are Elizabethan pork cooked in a casserole of cider and rosemary, salmon goujons served with a lime and ginger dip, grilled peppers stuffed with Mediterranean risotto, game pie in red wine, and spinach and feta goujons with tomato chutney. There is a good choice of sandwiches and ploughman's.

Regular real ales in this freehouse are Adnams Best Bitter and Regatta, Greene King IPA, Charles Wells Bombardier and Theakston Old Peculier, plus guest ales.

The pub is open all day, with food served from 12 noon to 7 pm except on Sundays, when it is 12 noon to 2 pm. Bookings for lunch are advisable on summer weekends. Telephone: 01603 667423.

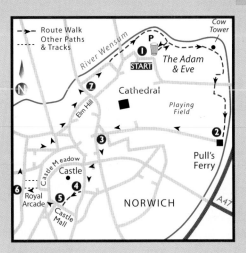

The Walk

① From the pub go through the car park and turn right alongside the river. The path bends right by Cow Tower, built in 1398-9 to strengthen the city's medieval defences. Pass to the right of the Red Lion and go across the road onto a paved path. Norwich School playing fields are on the right with the soaring cathedral spire behind.

② At the much-photographed medieval watergate of Pull's Ferry, turn right along Ferry Lane into the Cathedral Close.

③ Walk straight ahead through Ethelbert Gate and turn left on Upper King Street. With the Anglia TV headquarters facing you, turn right, cross Bank Plain and turn left to the Boer War memorial depicting the angel of peace sheathing the sword of war, then ahead down Market Avenue with the old Shirehall, now a museum, on your right.

④ Just before the entrance to an underground car park, turn right through a stone arch into the Castle Gardens. The path bends left past a small outdoor theatre

Norwich School playing fields

then zigzags left up to the higher level of the gardens, where there are good views over the city. Head diagonally right to come out on Farmers Avenue, opposite the glass entrance to Castle Mall.

⑤ Turn right past the Bell Hotel and right again on Castle Meadow. Cross the road then turn left through a large concrete arch and ahead into the Royal Arcade. This art nouveau gem, built in 1899, was described as 'a fragment of Arabian Nights dropped into the heart of the old city'.

⑥ Turn right on Gentleman's Walk, keep straight ahead into Exchange Street then turn right into Bedford Street. Turn left down St Andrew's Hill, cross St Andrew's Street and turn right into Princes Street. Soon turn left into Elm Hill, one of Norwich's oldest and most picturesque streets.

⑦ At the end turn left and, just before Fye Bridge, right on Quay Side, past old warehouses. Cross the road and continue on Riverside Walk with the courts on your right, through large metal gates and then turn right into the car park by the pub.

PLACES OF INTEREST NEARBY

The Castle Museum is reopening in spring 2001 after an £11.8 million refurbishment which will reveal parts of the castle not seen by the public before. There will be a new archaeology gallery to tell the story of Queen Boudicca and display major Iceni treasures, and a new art gallery to house exhibitions from the Tate. The castle itself is 900 years old, built as a royal palace, becoming the county gaol and later still a museum. Its stone keep is recognised as one of the finest Norman buildings in Europe. Check opening times by telephoning 01603 493625.

Surlingham
The Coldham Hall Tavern

MAP: OS LANDRANGER 134 (GR 325072)   **WALK 25**   **DISTANCE:** 3½ MILES

DIRECTIONS TO START: SURLINGHAM IS 6 MILES SOUTH-EAST OF NORWICH AND REACHED BY ONE OF SEVERAL MINOR ROADS OFF THE A146. FROM BRAMERTON, FOLLOW SIGNS FOR SURLINGHAM FERRY, THEN TURN RIGHT ON THE COMMON TOWARDS SURLINGHAM VILLAGE. COLDHAM HALL IS THEN SIGNED LEFT DOWN A LANE.
PARKING: IN THE PUB CAR PARK.

The River Yare meanders through a varied landscape as it heads for the sea – wide open marshland with enormous skies as it nears Yarmouth but here, closer to Norwich, leafier and more secret. On a midweek day out of high season you could almost be on a stretch of the upper Amazon. No parrots of course, except that the pub has an African grey called Pepé who calls out to customers from his cage behind the bar. This is a good walk for birds of the native species, too, as it passes through the domain of the heron and marsh harrier, which can often be seen drifting low over the reedbeds, and then later takes in a variety of river wildfowl and a couple of hides looking out over pools fringed with vegetation where hidden warblers sing.

The Coldham Hall Tavern

When Queen Anne once sailed down the River Yare, she alighted at this point and asked for a meal of cold ham. It sounds an unlikely explanation for the pub's name but the villagers swear by it and certainly the good Queen could hardly have picked a more attractive spot to come ashore than this mellow redbrick and thatched house at the water's edge.

The Coldham Hall Tavern has an easygoing 'ask us and we'll do our best to give it you' atmosphere. There is rather more than cold ham on offer nowadays, as the pub serves an adventurous range of food in its beamed bars and restaurant, which are dominated by a huge brick fireplace. The standard menu has traditional favourites such as Lowestoft cod in batter and chargrilled steaks but then there's a whole row of specials blackboards that may offer Spanish paella, grilled skate with pink peppercorn and brandy sauce or duckling à l'orange. Mexican, Indian and French dishes are often featured, and there is a 'lite bite' range of baguettes with hot beef, pork, turkey or tuna melt, plus a children's menu. The pub is closed on Mondays from the end of November to the end of February.

This freehouse has Greene King IPA and Woodforde's Wherry as its real ales, with regular guests, plus Caffreys, John Smith's Extra Smooth, Stella, Foster's, Guinness and Strongbow.

Outside there is a large riverside garden and patio, and free overnight mooring for boat parties eating in the pub. Telephone: 01508 538591.

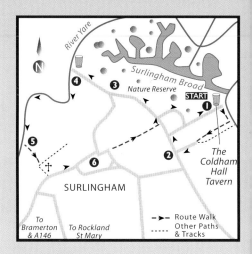

The Walk

① Go through the car park, with the pub behind you, passing Coldham Hall Sailing Club on your left. Turn right on a delightful grassy track, with Herons Marsh on your left. A heron is, indeed, quite likely to appear, and I was treated to a view of an aerial skirmish between a marsh harrier and a crow determined to see off the bigger bird. Follow the path through grazing marsh to the road.

② Turn right and keep straight ahead out of the village on the lane flanked by drifts of white cow parsley in spring, a sight of which the good Queen would have approved according to one of its more evocative country names – Queen Anne's lace.

③ At a junction, bear right on Ferry Road following a sign to Surlingham Ferry. After the lane narrows between trees, walk into the grounds of the Ferry House pub (another pleasant spot to sit outside) and turn immediately left following a half-hidden fingerpost to the river.

The River Yare at Coldham Hall

④ Turn left on the river bank and go over a stile on a 'permissive path'. Follow the river as it twists and turns, passing a nature reserve with two hides, the second dedicated to the memory of popular naturalist and writer Ted Ellis. The vegetation is regularly cut back, but the going is slightly rough at times.

⑤ The path bends left away from the river and leads uphill between overhanging hedges. Bear left on the lane, passing the pretty, round-towered church of St Mary. There are 200 similar church towers in Norfolk and Suffolk, though they are rare in the rest of Britain. At the T-junction turn left then, shortly, bear left again up Pratts Hill.

⑥ At the top, turn right on New Road, which bends sharply left, and after 100 yards keep straight ahead on a pleasant footpath into open country. When this meets the road, turn left and after 50 yards right following a public bridleway sign. This track bends to the right to meet Coldham Hall Carnser, the lane you drove up originally. Turn left back to the pub.

PLACES OF INTEREST NEARBY

Surlingham Church Marsh is a nature reserve with free admission at all times. It has a pleasant 1¼-mile nature trail and hides, with birds and plants of reed and sedge fen, ditches and open water. Turn left at the lane at the end of Coldham Hall Carnser and keep on through the village – the reserve is on the left.

Strumpshaw Fen is an RSPB reserve on the other side of the river approached via the A47 through Brundall. There are several hides, including a tower hide with a fine view over the reserve, and apart from its many bird species Strumpshaw is noted for its swallowtail butterflies in season. Open daily from dawn to dusk.

Claxton

The Beauchamp Arms

MAP: OS LANDRANGER 134 (GR 350044)   **WALK 26**   **DISTANCE:** 2½ MILES

DIRECTIONS TO START: CLAXTON IS 8 MILES SOUTH-EAST OF NORWICH, REACHED BY ONE OF SEVERAL MINOR ROADS OFF THE A146. THE PUB IS JUST TO THE EAST OF CLAXTON VILLAGE, DOWN A WELL-SIGNED DRIVEWAY. **PARKING:** IN THE PUB CAR PARK (NOT ON THE GRASSY AREA OUTSIDE, WHERE THERE IS A CHARGE).

B oats and big skies are two of the typical features of the Norfolk scene that spring to many people's minds, and this walk has them both in good measure. Through a vast expanse of grazing marsh criss-crossed by drainage dykes, where swans nest and herons stand sentinel, and then on a raised path beside the broad River Yare, there is a feeling of space and openness here that lifts the spirits. The Beauchamp Arms itself stands on a site known to the Romans and where later the Buckenham ferry crossing was busy for several hundred years, well into the last century. The river was a vital commercial link between Norwich and Yarmouth, and from there across to mainland Europe, but nowadays only pleasure boats pass up and down between its reed-fringed banks.

The Beauchamp Arms

This large, stylish freehouse, named after a long-established local family, was built in 1901 on the site of an earlier inn that burned down, and it is easy to imagine it as the setting for weekend parties of Edwardian ladies and gentlemen making their way by boat from Norwich or by train to Buckenham and then across the ferry. The patio makes an ideal spot for the gentle pastime of river-watching, whether intricate boat manoeuvres or the graceful dive of a great crested grebe. But it is no hardship to be forced indoors by the weather as the recently-refurbished pub offers a warm, comfortable and family-friendly welcome.

There is a wide choice of home-cooked food, with fish a speciality. Skate wing, shark steak with Cajun seasoning, and bouillabaisse of fresh fish, prawns and mussels in wine are among the dishes on offer. There is also a range of house speciality pies, including Old English lamb pie with Victoria plums and a minty sauce, and turkey and mussel pie in a curry sauce. Four or five veggie dishes are always on offer and there is a children's menu.

Woodforde's Wherry is the house bitter and there are always two more real ales – Woodforde's Great Eastern is another favourite.

There is a pool room, a play area for children outside and a box of toys inside. Camping facilities are available and there are five guest rooms, including two family rooms. Telephone: 01508 480247.

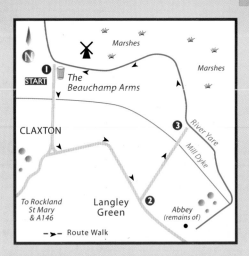

The Walk

① From the pub, head back down the tree-lined drive towards the road. Where the drive forks, turn left to meet the lane and then left again. There is a blind right-hand bend ahead, so it is probably better to walk on the grass verge on the left. There is now a lovely open view towards the river and one of those surreal images of boats sailing serenely over the fields.

② After a modern terrace of houses on the right, turn left down a broad track directly opposite Maple House, No 38. The path leads between hedges and when it opens out, you might well see Egyptian geese, one of the more colourful of the introduced bird species and now fairly common in Norfolk. A vital part of the county's economy is also clearly visible on the right, in the shape of the British Sugar factory at Cantley. If you are unlucky enough to have the wind from the east, you might experience the peculiar caramelised fish smell that is a byproduct of the beet processing. Fortunately the production season, or 'campaign' as they call it locally, lasts only from late October to February.

A typical Norfolk scene

③ When you reach the river, climb a stile and turn left along the river bank. Across the water the reedbeds of Buckenham Marshes stretch away to higher ground and trains potter along to Yarmouth. The path now follows the river all the way back and you are quite likely to meet cows, though they are well used to people and will ignore you as you pass.

Not far from the pub there is a short, tricky stretch where a raised girder rail runs alongside the path. Normally you walk to the right of the rail but if the river has been high, this could be too boggy for comfort. If so, turn left just before the rail, down the bank and right along the field edge. After about 100 yards go up the bank again to climb a stile over a wooden fence and back to the pub.

PLACES OF INTEREST NEARBY

Raveningham Hall Gardens, 4 miles north-west of Beccles off the B1136, are noted plantsman's gardens laid out at the beginning of the 20th century with a fine collection of rare shrubs and herbaceous plants. There is a Victorian conservatory, a walled garden and a commercial nursery. The gardens are open in May, June and July on Sundays and Bank Holiday Mondays and also Easter Sunday and Monday. Telephone 01508 548222.

Pettitts Animal Adventure Park, off the B1140 between Reedham and Acle (from Claxton, approach via the Reedham car ferry) is a family-orientated attraction with animals including Falabella horses, wallabies and tame goats, chickens and ducks. There's an adventure play area with ball pond and giant snake slide, a half-mile railway, vintage car ride and astroglide. Open Sunday to Friday and August Bank Holiday Saturday. Telephone: 01493 701403.

Walcott
The Lighthouse Inn

MAP: OS LANDRANGER 133 (GR 359319)	**WALK 27**	DISTANCE: 3½ MILES

DIRECTIONS TO START: WALCOTT IS ON THE B1159 COAST ROAD 5 MILES FROM NORTH WALSHAM. THE PUB IS JUST SOUTH OF THE VILLAGE BY THE SIDE OF THE MAIN ROAD. **PARKING:** IN THE PUB CAR PARK, WITH PERMISSION.

Walcott is one of only three Celtic place names in Norfolk, along with Eccles and Lynn – Walcote is the Celtic spelling and means 'village by the wood'. There's not much sign of woodland nowadays but every sign, on this walk, of the sea's unrelenting and so far largely unstoppable power. At nearby Happisburgh (pronounced, in thoroughly Norfolk fashion, Hazeborough) homes have been dropping over the edge of the cliff for years, and coastal erosion goes steadily onwards. The clifftop section of the walk provides clear evidence of the way the sea is reclaiming land, while flooding along Walcott seafront is a regular occurrence. In this holiday area there are, appropriately, two 'sticks of rock' – one in All Saints' church, which sells its own named variety in a spirit of enterprise that no doubt helped it to 'highly commended' status in the Tourist Church of the Year award, and the other in the form of the striking red and white striped Happisburgh lighthouse.

The Lighthouse Inn

This is a very friendly, unpretentious pub with a strong family feel. Built as a farmhouse around 1850, it passed through several brewery chains from the 1960s before being bought as a freehouse. The lighthouse of the name must be Happisburgh, just visible through trees beyond Walcott church.

There are two homely bars where dogs are allowed, a dining room with no-smoking area, a family room also used by walkers, a covered patio and a large, sunny beer garden.

The Lighthouse prides itself on freshly prepared value-for-money food using local ingredients. Homemade pies – always steak and kidney with another on the blackboard – are a speciality. Local crab and a variety of fish dishes change daily depending on availability.

A 'Wonders of the World' section features such dishes as chicken tikka masala, lamb rogan josh and vegetable balti, and there is always a good choice of vegetarian food. From April to the end of December the pub serves food from from 11 am to 10.30 pm; from January to March there is food all day at weekends and from 11 am to 2.30 pm and 6 pm to 10.30 pm on weekdays.

Adnams Best Bitter and Tetley cask-conditioned are the regular real ales, plus two guests such as Adnams Broadside and Morrells IPA.

The pub has a range of special events, including a fireworks display around Bonfire Night, a charity marquee weekend with live music in July and a barbecue with children's entertainment on Tuesday and Thursday nights in summer. Telephone: 01692 650371.

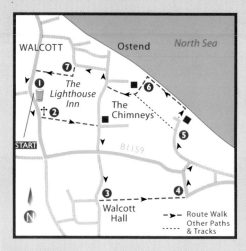

The Walk

① Turn left out of the pub and down the footpath by the roadside to All Saints' church. This is yet another big, airy Norfolk church, whose lofty 15th century tower has one of the best examples of decorated battlements in the country.

② Go through the churchyard and take a footpath at the far end with a green Happisburgh Circular Walk arrow leading between crop fields. At the lane turn right and then cross the main road to take a byroad. Happisburgh church and light-house are now prominent to the left.

③ At Walcott Hall farm turn left opposite a lane to pass between old and new barns, following a yellow waymarker. Walk along the field edge, through a gap into the next field and, after 100 yards, take a path diagonally left heading straight for the church. Go over a wooden bridge and straight across the next field.

④ Turn left at the lane and after a few yards straight ahead on the main road. When this bends sharply left, take a lane to

Happisburgh church and lighthouse seen from across the fields

the right and, after a short distance, turn left on a gravel track with fine views of the church and sea beyond.

⑤ Ignore a green arrowed path to the left and head straight for the sea, passing a Happisburgh Coast Watch mobile building. Turn left on the clifftop, past World War II pillboxes where wheatears can often be seen flitting around. The next stretch of path is pleasant, with the sea crashing against breakwaters below, but is unfenced and not a place to let young children run ahead.

⑥ Some 200 yards before houses, turn left following a green arrow and go right at the next multiple waymarker post on a grassy track to the lane. Turn right and follow the lane as it bends left.

⑦ Where the lane takes a sharp right-hander, turn left on a fingerposted path which bends right to the main road. Turn left along the field edge (or on the road if the path is overgrown) back to the pub.

PLACES OF INTEREST NEARBY

The Museum of the Broads in historic buildings at The Staithe at Stalham, 4 miles south of Walcott, tells how the mystery of their creation (medieval peat diggings) was solved and presents traditional Broads industries such as thatching, reed cutting, boat building, sail and rope making and eel catching with the tools needed for them. It also houses the steam launch Falcon, an ice yacht and the only concrete dinghy ever built. The museum is open daily from Easter to the end of October 10 am to 4 pm. Telephone: 01692 581681.

Norfolk Motorcycle Museum at Station Yard, Norwich Road, North Walsham, has a collection of motorcycles from the 1920s to the 1960s and is open daily from 10 am to 4.30 pm. Telephone: 01692 406266.

Potter Heigham
The Falgate Inn

MAP: OS LANDRANGER 134 (GR 414190) **WALK 28** **DISTANCE:** 3½ MILES

DIRECTIONS TO START: POTTER HEIGHAM (PRONOUNCED HIGH-EM) IS 12 MILES NORTH-EAST OF NORWICH. COMING FROM THAT DIRECTION ON THE A1062, THE PUB IS ON THE RIGHT AT THE ENTRANCE TO THE VILLAGE. **PARKING:** IN THE PUB CAR PARK, WITH PERMISSION.

To get a proper idea of the Norfolk Broads you really have to be in a boat, as very few footpaths go along the shores of these reed-fringed medieval lakes – a fact that tends to surprise visitors on walking holidays. This walk does at least offer tantalising glimpses of the largest broad, Hickling, which was dug out for peat around 700 years ago, but its main attractions are the wide open spaces of grazing marshland and swaying reedbeds with their abundance of wildlife. Grey herons are almost a certainty and the sight of a marsh harrier buffeted by the breeze is, thankfully, no longer the rarity it was only a few years ago.

Potter Heigham itself is a busy, 'boaty' place whose name is believed to derive from the potteries that thrived here in Roman times. It also achieved some literary fame last century for its role in Arthur Ransome's Broads-based novels *Coot Club* and *The Big Six*.

The Falgate Inn

'Abandon all hope who enter here', reads an inscription in Latin above the door of the pub. This is not a comment on the welcome you will receive, which is warm and friendly, but dates from when the local undertaker had his business here at the turn of the last century while his wife ran the pub. The legend on the pub sign – 'This gate hang high and hinder none, refresh and pay and travel on' – is a more fitting message nowadays for the many visitors to this busy Broads village.

The Falgate was built in 1886 and its name probably refers to tolls that were collected here by the estate on whose land it stood. It was gutted by fire in 1993 but rebuilt to retain its character, with a cosy, beamed bar and large brick fireplace, non-smoking dining room, family room – even an undercover store place for bikes and canoes and a drying room for fishermen.

Freshly-cooked traditional pub food, with an emphasis on fish and steaks, is the aim here. The regular menu has dishes such as whole lemon sole, Guinness steak and kidney pie and moules marinières, while the daily specials board could be offering pork steak in cider and cinnamon sauce, crab chowder or haddock in wild mushroom sauce.

Regular real ales are Tetley cask-conditioned and Greene King IPA, with at least one other guest in summer. There is a beer garden and overnight accommodation in five guest rooms, two of them ensuite. Telephone: 01692 670003.

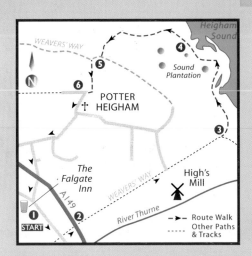

The Walk

① Turn right out of the pub and walk along Bridge Road. For a short detour to the famous medieval bridge on the River Thurne, keep straight ahead, but the walk turns left on a public footpath following a Weavers' Way marker, just before a large store car park on the right. After 300 yards cross the A149 and keep straight ahead on a broad track.

② There is grazing marsh all around now, where the scratchy song of sedge warblers is common. In the many dykes criss-crossing the marsh, flowers of yellow water-lily stick up in summer like golden lollipops. Ahead and to the right can be seen the ten turbines of the West Somerton windfarm.

③ When the track bends right, cross a wooden bridge to the left and immediately turn left, still following the Weavers' Way. The masts of boats on Heigham Sound can now be seen poking out of the reeds to the right. The grassy path leads over a stile and through hedge 'tunnels' before opening out with woodland on the left.

One of the many dykes that cut across the grazing marsh

④ There are wild roses everywhere along this stretch in season, and electric blue damselflies and red admiral butterflies to keep you company. A landing stage a few yards off the path to the right gives views over the open water of Hickling Broad. Pass a birdwatching hide and follow the path as it bends round to the left with more views over the broad.

⑤ After about 400 yards turn left across a wooden bridge, following a Norfolk County Council circular walk sign, while the Weavers' Way continues ahead. The path goes through birch woodland to a stile. Climb this, turn right and after 200 yards, at a junction of paths, turn right again, still following the green arrow sign.

⑥ At the lane turn left to the handsome, largely 14th century church of St Nicholas with its thatched roof and round flint tower. Turn right on Church Road, passing a clay barn on the left. Turn left on Station Road, cross the A149 and at the T-junction turn right on Ludham Road to the pub.

PLACES OF INTEREST NEARBY

How Hill, signed off the A1062 at Ludham, west of Potter Heigham, is a beautiful spot overlooking the River Ant that is part nature reserve, part Broads museum. It includes Toad Hole Cottage, a quaint former eelcatcher's home that now offers a fascinating glimpse of Victorian country life. This is open Easter to May, and October, 11 am to 5 pm; June to September 10 am to 6 pm. There is also a wildlife trail open the same hours as the cottage and a water trail on an Edwardian-style electric boat called the Electric Eel. This runs from How Hill Staithe every hour on the hour at weekends, bank holidays and half-terms from Easter to May and in October; also June to September daily 10 am to 5 pm. Telephone: 01692 678763.

Winterton-on-Sea
The Fisherman's Return

MAP: OS LANDRANGER 134 (GR 494194) | **WALK 29** | **DISTANCE:** 3½ MILES

DIRECTIONS TO START: WINTERTON IS JUST OFF THE B1159 COAST ROAD ABOUT 7 MILES NORTH OF GREAT YARMOUTH. THE PUB IS IN THE CENTRE OF THE VILLAGE ON A STREET CALLED THE LANE. **PARKING:** IN THE PUB CAR PARK.

Life in Winterton has long been dominated by the sea – a livelihood for fishermen in years gone by and a draw nowadays for visitors from the holiday parks further down the coast – but there is no sign of it until you head up through the sheltering line of dunes onto the broad, sandy beach. This walk, too, has a deceptive start, taking in streets of attractive cottages and passing the soaring church tower before heading into the nature reserve – often a peaceful sun-trap in summer. Only when you breach the sand barrier do you get an idea of the power of the North Sea as it crashes onto the beach at Winterton Ness. The next stretch can be slow going, though there is usually hard sand to walk on, depending on the state of the tide. It is, however, possible to head off the beach at several points and take one of many paths heading back through the dunes reserve to the village.

The Fisherman's Return

Robinson Crusoe author Daniel Defoe recorded that he found the village of Winterton half built from the timbers of wrecked ships, and this attractive 300-year-old pub quite likely has such an origin. Popular with locals and holidaymakers alike, it has a cosy beamed and wood-panelled lounge bar, larger public bar and small dining room whose walls are covered in old photographs of fishermen and sailing boats.

Separate from the main building is the quaintly-named Tinho, a large tin-roofed wooden construction dating from around a century ago and used as a dining room for passengers on horse-drawn carriages and later charabancs who came out from Yarmouth on day trips. It is now used as a family room and there is a good-sized beer garden beyond.

Fish dishes feature strongly on the standard menu and daily specials board, among them a medley of fresh salmon and plaice in a garden herb sauce; monkfish coated in a mild curry sauce on a rice and spinach base; and fish pie of cod and prawns topped with potato and cheese. Local crab with salad is a favourite, as is orange tarragon chicken, and vegetarian dishes include aubergine and mushroom stroganoff and spinach cannelloni on a tomato base.

The regular real ale in this freehouse is Woodforde's Wherry and there are usually three guests – Morland Old Speckled Hen and Bombardier from Charles Wells are frequent visitors. Around 20 wines are on offer, with guest wines on a blackboard. Overnight accommodation is also available. Telephone: 01493 393305.

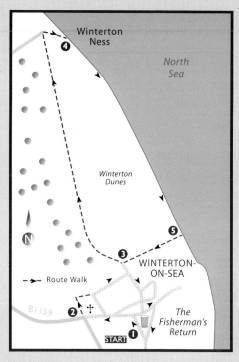

The Walk

① Turn right out of the pub on The Lane then left on Black Street to Holy Trinity and All Saints' church whose flint tower, dotted with wild yellow wallflowers in spring, dominates the landscape. It is the third highest church tower in Norfolk, behind Cromer and Wymondham, though local tradition says it is, in fact, 'a herring-and-a-half higher than Cromer'. Inside this largely 15th century church there is a unique Fishermen's Corner of nautical items created in the 1920s as a memorial to local men lost at sea.

② Go through the churchyard and turn right on a track, following a footpath sign between allotments. Turn right on a dirt track, left on North Market Road and ahead into Winterton Dunes nature reserve, one of the few areas of acid coastal

Winterton Ness

dune and heath left in northern Europe and an important wildlife habitat.

③ The sandy main path follows an arrow sign ahead, with a wire fence on your left, over the dunes. At a junction with a broader track, where there are concrete blocks and information boards, turn right to the sea and up onto the beach at Winterton Ness. This part of the coast looks innocuous on the map but currents make it a dangerous place once dreaded by sailors. Defoe gives a vivid picture of a disaster here one night in 1692 involving vessels from King's Lynn and Wells carrying corn, a fleet of ships from the north and colliers from Yarmouth; 200 ships and 1,000 lives were lost.

④ Turn right along the beach, eventually passing a roped-off nesting area for little terns, one of Britain's rarest seabirds and surely one of the most beautiful.

⑤ Turn up to a yellow diamond-shaped 'Telephone Cable' pole at the top of the beach, take a path aligned with the distant wind turbines ahead, then turn diagonally left towards a low, white building. Turn left into North Market Road, left on Beach Road, right on The Loke (a good old Norfolk name for a lane), right at the junction and almost immediately right into the pub car park.

PLACES OF INTEREST NEARBY

Hickling Broad, with a visitor centre reached by following the brown duck signs from Hickling village, north-west of Winterton-on-Sea, is a National Nature Reserve on Norfolk's largest and wildest broad. It offers boardwalk nature trails. The reserve is open all year round and the centre from April to September, 10 am to 5 pm. Guided boat trails run most days from June to September starting from the Pleasure Boat Inn at Hickling Staithe. To book telephone 01692 598276.

Burgh Castle
Church Farm

MAP: OS LANDRANGER 134 (GR 476051) **WALK 30** **DISTANCE:** 3¼ MILES

DIRECTIONS TO START: BURGH CASTLE IS 2 MILES OFF THE A143 JUST SOUTH-WEST OF GREAT YARMOUTH. GO STRAIGHT DOWN THE MAIN VILLAGE STREET, FOLLOWING A SIGN FOR CHURCH FARM AND THE CASTLE ITSELF. **PARKING:** IN THE LARGE PUB CAR PARK.

Tucked away round a corner from Yarmouth's flashing lights and fast-food bars, Burgh Castle commands an atmospheric position on rising ground above the estuary where the Yare and Waveney meet. The castle itself must be one of the finest – and perhaps among the least well-known – of Roman remains in Britain. Built around AD 280 as one of the so-called Forts of the Saxon Shore to protect south-east England from sea-borne raiders, it still has massive 15ft high walls of flint bonded with courses of tile on three sides of a 7-acre site.

The walk crosses the castle site, which in Roman times was much closer to the sea, taking in superb views from its open side and then heading down to the water's edge. It then follows part of the newly improved Angles Way alongside Breydon Water before cutting inland on quiet paths and lanes back to the village.

Church Farm

With no name board or sign hanging outside, Church Farm could be mistaken at first glance for the private country club it used to be. Once you are inside, however, in the beamed bar or dining room, this is a popular and friendly pub – and one with a superb setting hard to match anywhere in Norfolk. On a rise overlooking Breydon Water, it makes the most of its sunny position to be very much a family-orientated place with a large garden, well-equipped children's games room and bouncy castles in summer.

The core of the pub is the old farmhouse built next to the church of SS Peter and Paul in 1788. With modern extensions it opened as a club in the 1980s and later became a freehouse. In summer especially it is a lively place; a neighbouring caravan site with room for 140 tourers is part of the business, and the entertainment includes music and barbecues.

Among a wide range of food, fish is a speciality – fresh cod and sole from nearby Lowestoft as well as tuna and marlin from America. On the blackboard (daily except Sundays when there is a carvery) lobster thermidor is a summertime special and other dishes include beef in black bean and onion sauce, and moussaka and feta salad.

Real ales are Tetley cask-conditioned, Greene King Abbot and Morland Old Speckled Hen with regular guests.

Church Farm is open all day on Sundays, and there are six guest rooms. Telephone: 01493 780251.

The Walk

① Cross the lane outside the car park and go straight ahead on the track signed 'Broads Walk', heading for the castle. After 100 yards go through a wooden gate on the right and head diagonally across the fields to the long line of the castle walls. Pass through a gap into the grassed arena that was once the mighty Roman fort of Gariannonum and head diagonally left to the bottom corner of the site.

② Go down steps and turn immediately right on a footpath signed with the Broads Walk green arrow. Your view of the water is now blocked by tall, waving reeds but there are tantalising calls of wading birds and gulls to be heard and, just before Church Farm, you turn left to meet the river.

③ Turn right alongside the broad, glittering expanse of Breydon Water and you are now on the long-distance Angles Way, which runs from Yarmouth to the start of the Peddars Way at Knettishall Heath. There are usually scores of birds here, especially at low tide when waders

The Roman fort of Gariannonum

congregate to feed. Cormorants fly low over the water or perch on posts, their wings spread in heraldic pose. Across the water you can see the Berney Arms windmill and pub, which can be reached by boat or train, but not by road. The path is a pleasant one now as it follows the bends of the estuary with grazing marsh spread out below you.

④ Just before a small redbrick electricity building close to the water, turn right down the bank and head through a wooden gate on a gravel track. Shortly, at a junction of tracks, turn right and follow the path as it heads inland. There are views of Yarmouth away to the left across the marshes where horses graze and mute swans glide on the narrow channels.

⑤ Eventually the path passes between hedges to meet a quiet lane where you turn

right with occasional cottages on both sides. After ½ mile the lane bends left to the main road where you turn right and head back to the pub.

PLACES OF INTEREST NEARBY

Redwings Horse Sanctuary at Caldecott Hall, on the A143 just north of Fritton, has a large collection of rescued horses, ponies and donkeys that can be seen on paddock walks and gives displays of humane horse handling. The centre is open daily from Good Friday to the end of October, 10 am to 5 pm. Telephone: 01493 488638.

Fritton Lake Countryworld, just off the A143 south of Yarmouth, has woodland walks by the lake, an adventure playground, a falconry centre, heavy horses, a children's farm, miniature railway and golf. Open daily 10 am to 5.30 pm. Telephone: 01493 488208.